Teacher Guide

Play Like a Morning Star

*Play! Recorders in the Classroom
Volume 5 - Ensemble Music for Grades 6-8*

PLAY! RECORDERS IN THE CLASSROOM

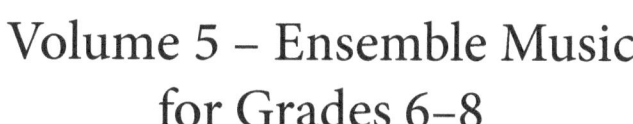

Volume 5 – Ensemble Music
for Grades 6–8

Play Like a Morning Star

by David Gable

TEACHER GUIDE

Printed with support from the Waldorf Curriculum Fund

Published by Waldorf Publications
at the Research Institute for Waldorf Education
351 Fairview Avenue, Suite 625
Hudson, NY 12534

Title: *Play Like a Morning Star*
   Volume 5 – Ensemble Music for Grades 6–8
   Play! Recorder Series for the Classroom
   Teacher Guide
Author/composer/arranger: David Gable
Editor: Patrice Maynard
Cover: Ella LaPointe
Proofreader: Ruth Riegel
Layout: Ann Erwin
© 2025 Waldorf Publications
ISBN#: 978-1-963686-06-7

Contents

About Using This Book

Part 1 - Music in Two Parts

1.	Amasee	14
2.	Dance Like a Butterfly	14
3.	Abiyo, Abeyo	15
4.	Jump Dance	15
5.	Johnny Grotto	16
6.	Sunrise Call	16
7.	Llywyn Onn (The Ash Grove)	17
8.	Tongo	17
9.	Halima Pakasholo	18
10.	Estampie	18
11.	Sing Hallelu!	19
12.	Ding Dong Diggidiggidong	19
13.	Santiana	19
14.	Mary Had a Baby	21
15.	Ma'oz Tzur	22
16.	Freu' Dich des Lebens!	22
17.	Love's Content	22
18.	Ad Cantus Laetitiae	23
19.	Te Solo Adoro	24
20.	Cupid Detected	24
21.	Lachend Kommt der Sommer	25
22.	Dundai	25
23.	La Adelita	25
24.	Envoyons de l'avant	26
25.	Dry Those Eyes	26
26.	Le Berger Fidèle	27

Part B - Music in Three Parts

27.	Te Aroha	29
28.	Mama Paquita	30
29.	Askari eee	30
30.	Chevaliers de la Table Ronde	30
31.	Sine Nomine	31
32.	Roll the Old Chariot Along	31
33.	Julia, Julia, Pela la Yuca	32

34.	Round and Round the Earth Is Turning	33
35.	Red Iron Ore	33
36.	Alla Matina (Bella Ciao)	34
37.	Cielito Lindo	35
38.	Au Chant de l'alouette	36
39.	Pastyme with Good Companye	36
40.	Ma Nishtana	37
41.	Dayenu	37
42.	Country Gardens	37
43.	Star in the East	38
44.	Ulele	39
45.	Aylesbury	39
46.	Blow Thy Horne, Hunter	39
47.	Cape Cod Girls	40
48.	All Joy to Great Caesar	40
49.	Jefferson and Liberty	41
50.	We Shall Overcome	42
51.	Gathering Peascods	42
52.	Kum Bachur Atzel	43
53.	Yankee Doodle	43
54.	The British Grenadiers	44
55.	We'll Rant and We'll Roar	44
56.	Ah Robin, Gentle Robin	45
57.	Palomita	46
58.	O Mitissima/Virgo Virginum/Haec Dies	46
59.	Wenn Ich Ein Vöglein Wär	48
60.	Pinks and Lilies	49
61.	Mi Y'malel	49
62.	Bigi Kaiman	49
63.	Miserere Nostri Domine	50
64.	All Into Service	51
65.	Boomba	51
66.	Troika	51
67.	A Southerly Wind and Cloudy Sky	52
68.	Shake the Papaya Down	52
69.	At Summer Morn	53
70.	Up and Down This World Goes Round	53
71.	Karaguna	54
72.	A Voyage to the Moon	54
73.	Shosholoza	55
74.	Honor to the Hills	56
75.	Marche pour Nérée	56
76.	We Be Three Poore Mariners	57
77.	Feldblumen	58

78.	Sonata Prima	59
79.	Were You There?	60
80.	The Echo	60

Part C - Music in Four Parts

81.	Kommt und Laßt Uns Tanzen	61
82.	Glaube und Hoffe!	61
83.	Da Pacem Domine	62
84.	Samba Lele	62
85.	Down, Down, Down	62
86.	Ha Ba Tshameka	63
87.	As I Mee Walked	63
88.	Ein Feste Burg Ist Unser Gott	64
89.	Schaut Hin! Dort Liegt im Finstern Stall	64
90.	El Corrido de Gregorio Cortez	65
91.	Lass Dein' Engel mit Mir Fahren	66
92.	Finlandia Hymn	67
93.	Go Down, Moses	68
94.	Nous Étions Trois Soldats	68
95.	Viva il Nostra Alcide	68
96.	Es Ist Ein' Ros' Entsprungen	69
97.	Nun Danket Alle Gott	69
98.	This Train	70
99.	Dem Bones	70
100.	Hot Time in the Old Town	71
101.	Levellers and Diggers	73
102.	By'm Bye	74
103.	Follow the Drinking Gourd	75
104.	Great Big Stars	75
105.	Michael, Row the Boat Ashore	76
106.	Watah Come a Me Eye	76
107.	Ben Venga il Pastor Mio	77
108.	Un Canadien Errant	78
109.	Galliarde	79
110.	La Jesusita	80
111.	Sit Down, Brother	80
112.	Strike the Bell/Click Go the Shears	80
113.	Ballet des Matelotz	83
114.	Vous, Saints Ministres du Signeur	83
115.	Leto Leta Concio	84
116.	El Vito	85
117.	Dalekaya i Blizkaya	85
118.	Andalla	85

119. Daylight: A Musical Expression	87
120. Clair de Lune	89
121. Oh, Watch the Stars	89
122. La Raspa	89
123. Joy and Thanksgiving after the Storm	90
124. Los Esqueletos	90
125. Jupiter Hymn	91
126. St Agnes Eve	91
127. Hymn to the Sun	92
128. Crazy Blues	94
129. Apart	94
130. It Was a Lover and His Lass	96
131. Ain't Gonna Let Nobody Turn Me Around	97
132. Shine Like a Morning Star	98
133. Saint Louis Blues	98
134. Magnetic Rag	99
135. Solace, A Mexican Serenade	100
136. Lift Every Voice and Sing	100
137. Charleston	100

Part D - Music in Five or More Parts

138. Alleluia	102
139. Galileo's Epitaph	102
140. Let's Have a Peale for John Cooke's Soule	104
141. Laudate Nomen	104
142. Jubilate Deo	105
143. Sumer Is Icumin In	105
144. Joy in the Gates of Jerusalem	106
145. Sing We Now Merrily	107
146. Now Thanked Bee the Great God Pan	107
147. Thebana Bella	108
148. Jinkin the Jester	108
149. Now Is the Month of Maying	109
150. Pavane 'Le Bon Vouloir'	109
151. Canon 8 Parts: in 4. Retro & Retro	109
152. Largo, from Symphony No. 8 (From the *New World*)	110
153. Sinfonia à 5	112
154. Heigh Ho Holiday	113
155. Sing You Now After Me	113
156. Cantate Domino Omnis Terra	114

Appendices

Appendix A –	Finger Technique and Fingering Charts	115, 116
Appendix B –	Breathing	117
Appendix C –	Intonation	117
Appendix D –	Embouchure and Tonguing	118
Appendix E –	The Tenor and Bass Recorders	118
Appendix F –	Indices	119
	Geographical Index	
	Thematic Index	
Acknowledgments		124

About Using This Book

Volume 5 of the *Play! Recorders in the Classroom* series is organized differently than the preceding volumes. Rather than being sequenced by new skills, the music in this book is organized by the number of separate parts. Part A consists of music in two parts; Part B has music in three parts; Part C includes music in four parts; and Part D has an assortment of pieces in five or more parts. A quick glance will show that many of the pieces included have more staves than the indicated number of parts. This occurs when one of the voices can be performed on more than one type of recorder. Braces have been used to show parts that are doubled. It is admissible to perform such pieces with both of the doubled lines, though it is important to adjust numbers for balance. For example, if a piece is indicated as being playable with SAT (soprano, alto, and tenor) or SAB (soprano, alto, and bass), both tenor and bass instruments can be used, but they should not overbalance either of the other parts.

Classes that have progressed through the skills (or even most of the skills) presented in Volume 4 will have acquired enough fluency to be able to play many pieces of music, despite not having learned the highest and most difficult notes on the soprano, alto, and tenor recorders. Many of the pieces in Volume 5 will be playable by students that have learned only notes in the closed-thumb and open-thumb range. Most others will only require a few partial-thumb fingerings. Few of the selections in Volume 5 require the full range of notes presented in the first four volumes.

Children grow at different rates, and this means that one cannot assume that students in a particular grade level will be able, or unable, to begin playing the larger tenor and bass recorders. Some sixth graders are able to play tenor and bass, while some eighth graders (and even some adults) are not. In addition, one cannot assume that every school or class has access to the larger and more expensive instruments. Most of the music in Volume 5 is arranged with flexible instrumentation that usually includes tenor and bass, but which in many cases can also be performed without these instruments. Instrumentation options are indicated below the title of each piece. The method I used to do this warrants some explanation:

- the subheading "any combination of…" means that all of the parts may be played on any of the indicated instruments;
- "with optional bass" generally means that the bass is doubling another voice, usually the tenor. It may also indicate that the bass line, while adding harmonic support, is not entirely essential and may be omitted;
- a brace to the left of the staves indicates that the enclosed lines are essentially the same. There may be octave transpositions, but these will not have significant impact on the sound;
- the use of the word "or" (as in "SAT or SAB") shows that the indicated parts are interchangeable;
- the use of a semi-colon between instrumentation options (as in SAT; SAB) indicates that although the indicated parts are interchangeable, the

first option is preferable. This is often because while the part is playable on either instrument, it is significantly more difficult on one than on the other.

Some examples will help clarify: "Follow the Drinking Gourd" (#103) has the indication "SATB; SAB; or SAT." This means that, although the piece will sound best played with soprano, alto, tenor, and bass instruments on their respective parts, it will also be satisfactory if played with just soprano, alto, and bass or with soprano, alto, and tenor. "Blow Thy Horn, Hunter" (#46) in marked "SAB or STB; SA or ST." This indicates that the middle voice (marked A/T) can be played on either alto or tenor (or both, providing balance of voices is preserved). It also can be played without the bass part without greatly compromising the harmonies and voicing.

In general, music in each part of this volume is presented with the easier pieces first and the harder ones last. There are, however, three significant caveats to this. First, music is not necessarily of equal difficulty for all instruments involved. Second, there is a certain amount of subjective judgment involved in assessing a piece's difficulty. Third, some pieces have been positioned where they are because of page turn and space considerations. To help teachers avoid choosing a piece that goes beyond the current range of their students, for most pieces I have indicated the pitch range of each part to the left of the clef in the first system. However, range is not the only determining factor in assessing difficulty. It is hoped that by the time students are working with this volume they will have learned forked fingerings (introduced in Vol. 2), open-thumb fingerings (also introduced in Vol. 2), and partial-hole (aka half-hole) fingerings (introduced in Vol. 3). If not, teachers should pay attention to how many new fingerings might be required for a specific piece. Older students can generally handle more than one new technique at a time, but it is still a good idea not to present too many at once. There is one piece in this volume that uses a note not addressed in any of the previous volumes; #148, "Jinkin the Jester," reaches high B, which will be unfamiliar to students playing C instruments (Ø/12O/45OO).

In earlier volumes I included lyrics for many of the folk songs. In this volume I have mostly limited the inclusion of lyrics to selected rounds and to pieces in which the words relate specifically to curricular themes. Many of the selections in this volume were originally written as instrumental works and have no text whatsoever. Lyrics for the traditional songs in this volume are easily found online by searching for the title plus the word "lyrics."

An additional change in this volume is the use of breath marks. In pieces where the logical breathing points are self-evident, I have not put in breath marks. I have included them in pieces in which the phrases are not as easily discerned.

In recorder music, a small "8" is sometimes printed above the clef, indicating that the music sounds an octave higher than written. This is common with parts written specifically for soprano or bass recorders. I have omitted this "8" when a line can be performed as written by soprano and either alto or tenor.

In the notes I often refer to C recorders and F recorders. In the recorder world, these distinctions are different than in the world of orchestral wind instruments. Recorders are not transposing instruments, except for the octave indications mentioned above. C recorders simply have C as the lowest note, and F recorders have F as the lowest note. C recorders are the soprano (sometimes called the descant) and the tenor. F recorders are the alto, the bass, and the sopranino. Alto recorders are sometimes referred to as "treble" recorders, a designation which can be confusing because soprano, alto, tenor, and sopranino recorders all use the treble clef. The use of the word *treble* in this context basically means that the treble recorder (alto, in F) is largely in the range of treble singers.

It is my intention and hope that at least some of the music in this volume will be useful not only in the middle/intermediate school years, but also in high school and beyond. Several of the pieces at the end of each section, which may be too challenging for middle schoolers, have been included with this in mind.

PART A - Music in Two Parts

With the exception of Estampie (10), all of the selections in Part A can be performed using varied instruments. Many are call-and-response songs which were chosen for the express purpose of introducing students to the larger tenor and bass instruments.

1. Amasee - *African-American dance tune*
(any combination of S, A, T, and B)

The call-and-response format is quite common in traditional dances around the world. In "Amasee," the caller sings instructions for the dance, and the dancers and onlookers respond by singing *amasee, amasee*. Amasee is a dialect pronunciation of "I must see," and to my knowledge has no connection to anything in the dance itself.

Both parts in "Amasee" can be played on any type of recorder, though they are most easily played on the alto. Instruments may be freely mixed. Both parts are also quite easy on C recorders and bass. The response, using only the notes C, D, and E (all of which use only left hand fingers on F recorders), is particularly useful in helping students get accustomed to playing bass. Students playing the response must count rests carefully because the calls begin on beat 4.

2. Dance Like a Butterfly - *Cameroonian call and response*
(any combination of S, A, T, and B)

This is a children's action song from the Republic of Cameroon in west central Africa. As an activity or song it is too "young" for middle schoolers, but for learning to play a new instrument or for practicing reading it is very useful.

The song has a range of five notes. Played on C recorders, both call and response use only fingers of the top hand. On F recorders, both call and response are useful for practicing the bottom hand fingerings for G, A, and B, as well as the top hand fingerings for C and D. Both the call and the response are playable on any type of recorder, and instruments may be freely mixed.

3. Abiyo, Abeyo - *Aboriginal Australian call and response*
(any combination of S, A, T, and B)

This is a song of greeting. Consisting of the notes G, A, B, and D, both call and response are easy to play on both C and F recorders. The rhythms in the second line are tricky. In particular, the timing of the sixteenth notes in measures 5 and 6 will challenge some students. As with the previous songs, any type of recorder may be used for both call and response, and instruments may be mixed.

Students should already be familiar with dotted rhythms. This piece has double dots at the end. In this notation, the second dot adds half the value of the first dot.

4. Jump Dance - *Chahta nation call and response*
(any combination of S, A, and T, with optional B)

The music for this traditional indigenous dance is recorded in the book *Choctaw[1] Music and Dance*, by James H. Howard and Victoria Lindsay Levine, published in 1990 by the University of Oklahoma Press. In a Chahta jump dance song, the leader sings calls that vary somewhat from one to the next, while the responses are all the same and are typically derived from some portion of the initial call. The jump dance is also called a "stomp dance," and exists in many variants.

Using the notes G, A, C, D, and E, the calls require the use of the open thumb hole for the two highest notes when played on C recorders. The response phrases, using only G, A, and C, are ideal for introducing students to tenor and bass instruments. I have given the call line to soprano, alto, and/or tenor instruments only because the quick rhythms will not speak easily on the bass. The response part may be played on any type of recorder, and instruments may be mixed.

Student who try to play by ear may be challenged by the subtle differences between measure 2 and measure 4. This jump dance also features meter changes, which may be a new idea to many students. The length of the quarter notes remains constant throughout the piece.

The Chahta are an indigenous people of the southeastern woodlands, in the area that is now Alabama and Mississippi. They sided with the Americans against the British in the War of 1812 and the Battle of New Orleans, yet many were forcibly removed to Indian Territory (now Oklahoma) and Louisiana in the early 1830s. During WWI, Chahta soldiers served as "codetalkers," transmitting messages using their native language.

---

1 Choctaw is the Anglicization of *Chahta*, the endonym of this indigenous people. The origin of the endonym is unknown, though it may derive from the Chahta phrase meaning "river people."

5. Johnny Grotto - *Trinidadian and Tobagonian call and response*
(any combination of S, A, and T, with optional B)

This traditional song from the Caribbean island nation of the Republic of Trinidad and Tobago tells of a fisherman's son who spends the entire night fishing.

The high G in measure 4 requires the use of the open thumb hole on F recorders and the partial thumb fingering on C recorders (Ø/123/OOOO).

I have given the call to soprano, alto, and/or tenor in this setting because the quick eighth-note rhythms will not speak easily on the bass recorder. Responses may be played on any type of recorder, and instruments may be mixed.

6. Sunrise Call - *Zuni call and response*
(SS, SA, ST, SB; TS, TA, TT, TB)

This is a portion of a Zuni song transcribed in 1904 by German-American composer Carlos Troyer. According to Troyer's notes, the "sun-priest" sang the call to rouse the people for the day. The Zuni are believed to have lived in the same region in the southwestern U.S. for 3,000 to 4,000 years. They are a branch of the Pueblo peoples, but their traditional language is a language isolate, a tongue with no recognized relationship to other languages. Linguists believe that Zuni has been spoken in largely its current form for as long as six or seven millennia.

I have listened to performances of this song played on Native American flute. It is typically ornamented in ways that cannot readily be expressed using standard music notation. Troyer's transcription and what appears here are mere approximations.

Note the difference between call and response in measures 6 and 8. Students attempting to play the response by ear will probably play F-A-A instead of D-F-F in measure 8. The alto and bass parts in measure 8 have been shifted up an octave to keep notes in the instruments' ranges. The original response voicing is heard in the S/T line.

The low Fs may make this piece difficult for some students to play on tenor recorder.

Students should already be familiar with dotted rhythms. This piece has double dots at the beginning and end. In this notation, the second dot adds half the value of the first dot.

7. Llywyn Onn (The Ash Grove) - Welsh folk song
(ST; SA)

First published in 1802, the melody for this Welsh song has been set to many lyrics ranging the religious to the bawdy. The song "Cease Your Funnin'" from *The Beggar's Opera* (1728) is remarkably similar both melodically and harmonically. Since music for *The Beggar's Opera* consisted primarily of folk songs arranged by Johann Christoph Pepusch (1667–1752), it seems quite likely that the melody of "The Ash Grove" may itself derive from an earlier song. One candidate is "Constant Billy," a Morris tune found in the 1665 edition of John Playford's *The Dancing Master*.

Both melody and harmony lie very comfortably on C recorders when played in G Major, but this unfortunately puts the harmony line too low for altos in just three places. The harmony line can be performed on alto by playing the parenthetical upper notes in measures 6, 11, and 22. This gives the altos F♯ as the lowest note. The ST setting is preferred, both because it maintains the parallel motion by thirds and because low F♯ uses an awkward partial-hole fingering on the alto (T/123/456Ø). It is also possible to use a combination of altos and tenors on the harmony line, as long as the harmony does not overpower the melody.

8. Tongo - Polynesian call and response
(any combination of S, A, T, and B)

Historically, Polynesian peoples were great sea-farers, traversing vast expanses of ocean in long canoes. Songs like "Tongo" served to coordinate the efforts of those paddling a vessel.

In this setting both call and response can be played on any recorder. Given the range of low A to high A, the figures are most easily played on the alto. On C recorders there are several places that cross the register break. This, however, also makes it a good piece for working on partial-thumb fingerings for soprano and tenor players.

The notes in "Tongo" are not especially difficult (despite the calls reaching high A), but there are some rhythmic pitfalls. Measures 2 and 5 have very similar melodic shapes, but the rhythm is not the same. In addition, the quarter rest at the end of the call in measure 7 makes it tempting for the response players to start measure 8 one beat too soon.

9. Halima Pakasholo - Namibian call and response
(SA, ST, SAT, SAB, STB, or SATB)

"Halima Pakasholo" is a song of greeting. The calls are easily played on C recorders, and the responses are easily played on all. Playing the calls on alto is difficult because of the partial-hole fingerings for C♯ and F♯. In this setting I have the bass part playing responses all the way through, meaning that the song cannot be played with just soprano and bass.

The lyrics are simple. Every call is *halima pakasholo*, and every response is *halima, halima*.

10. Estampie - 13th-century dance
(SA)

The estampie was a popular dance from from the 12th to 14th century. It probably originated in France, but it soon spread throughout most of Europe. It is not known how it was danced, but existing music suggests that it was structured and repetitive.

The music for an estampie consists of phrases (puncta) that begin in the same way and end differently. The end of the first punctus is called the apertum, meaning "open," and the mind of the second is called the clausum, meaning "closed." When teaching this kind of music, I find it helpful to compare the endings to punctuation: the apertum is like a comma, and the clausum is like a period. An estampie may have anywhere from five to seven sections.

This estampie is particularly interesting in that the two parts are written in different keys.[2] This avoids the harmonic clashes that would result from playing B♮ with F♮ or C♮ with F♯. There are other dissonances that occur throughout the piece, but the tritone (diminished fifth or augmented fourth) is so dissonant that musicians of the Renaissance called it the "diabolus en musica," or the "devil in music." In the 11th century, theorist Guido of Arezzo (c. 991 or 992–after 1033) cautioned against using the interval, though he did not use the later, more sinister-sounding term. It is worth noting that every punctus in this piece ends with an open fifth or octave. The major and minor chords that are a central feature of later tonal music were not part of medieval musical thought. Medieval composers preferred the clear resonant sound of the perfect intervals.

The individual sections of this estampie are not difficult to play, but keeping track of the often subtle changes from one phrase or section to the next can be

---

[2] I use the term "keys" somewhat loosely, since tonality as we perceive it today did not exist in the thirteenth century.

challenging. Students who play by ear or by rote rather than reading the music will have difficulty. Although the alto part is playable on tenor recorders, it will cross the register break several times in each punctus. Performance on soprano and alto instruments is preferable.

11. Sing Hallelu - *African-American spiritual*
(any combination of S, A, and T, with optional B)

This spiritual alternates narrative calls with the response "Sing Hallelu." It is most effective sung or played at a lively tempo. Lyrics vary from one version to another:

(call) *Mary had a \ baby,* \
(response) *sing halle-\lu!* \ (4x)

Subsequent verses follow the traditional form: *Where was he born? Born in a manger; What did she name him? Named him baby Jesus,* and so forth. For singing, rhythms need to be adjusted to fit the text.

The call line extends into the partial-thumb register for C recorders but goes too low for F instruments. The responses can be played on any instrument.

12. Ding Dong Diggidiggidong - *anonymous round in two parts*
(any combination of S, A, and T, with optional B)

Ding dong, diggidiggidong, \ *Diggidiggidong, the cat she's gone!* \ *Ding dong, diggidiggidong,* \ *Diggidiggi ding dang dong.*

This light-hearted round has been a favorite with many of my students, whether singing or playing instruments. In the key of F, as it is written here, it is easier to play on alto than on C recorders. I have simplified the rhythms for bass recorder because of its slower response. The frequent low Fs will be challenging to those playing bass and tenor recorders because they require the use of finger 7. Students with smaller hands may also have difficulty reaching finger 7 on alto recorders.

13. Santiana (The Plains of Mexico) - *capstan shanty*
(any combination of S, A, and T, with optional B)

A capstan is a machine that was used on sailing ships to raise the anchor and perform other heavy-lifting tasks. It consisted of a vertical cylindrical body around which the anchor chain or cables were wrapped, and into which long bars could be inserted. The crew would push on these bars to turn the capstan and pull on the chain or cable. If the capstan was large enough, the shantyman (the crew member who sang or played the shanty to help synchronize the efforts of the crewmen) might stand or sit on top of it.

"Santiana" is a misspelling of the name of Antonio López de Santa Anna, a military leader in the Mexican war of independence and Mexico's eighth president. The lyrics of the shanty tell of Santa Anna's exploits in the Mexican-American war. The text of the first verse and refrain are:

Verse
(call) *Oh! \ Santiana \ gained the day,*
(response) *A–\way, Santi-\ana!*
(call) *Na-\poleon of the \ West they say,*
(response) *A–\long the plains of \ Mexi-co.*

Refrain
(call) *Well, \ heave 'er up and a-\way we'll go,*
(response) *A–way, Santi-\ana! *
(call) *Heave 'er up and a-\way we'll go,*
(response) *A–\long the plains of \ Mexi-co.*

For singing, rhythms and articulations need to be adjusted to match the lyrics. I did not put slurs in the music because they make finger changes awkward, but the pairs of eighth notes in "along" and "Mexico" are slurred when singing the shanty.

Later verses incorrectly attribute to Santa Anna victories in battles of the Mexican-American War that were actually won by the U.S. Army under Zachary Taylor. The open adulation of a Mexican military leader in an English shanty seems unusual, and there is no direct evidence explaining it. However, the presence of two British-made steamships (the Guadalupe and the Moctezuma) with British captains and crews comprised largely of English sailors in the Mexican fleet during the Texas Revolution (1835–1836) suggests that the lyrics may have originated among the crews of these ships. Both ships suffered significant damage, and their crews suffered devastating losses of life, in naval battles against the Texan navy. There are many other sets of lyrics, some having nothing to do with either Santa Anna or the Mexican revolution. It was common for shantymen to improvise verses in order for the shanty to fill the time needed to complete the task.

This call-and-response song could have multiple curricular connections. As a sea shanty it could be associated with sailing and exploration. As a capstan shanty it could accompany the study of simple machines in a physics block. It could also support the study of U.S. and/or Mexican history or a study of political rebellion.

Part A – Music in Two Parts

The call line may be played on soprano, alto or tenor, and any type of recorder may be used for the responses. The low Fs at the end of both the call and response lines will be challenging to those playing bass and tenor recorders because they require the use of finger 7. Students with smaller hands may also have difficulty reaching finger 7 on alto recorders.

It is important to note at this point that the fingerings for bass recorder are not always the same as those for alto, despite the fingering charts that are commonly provided with an instrument. This is due to the bass instrument's larger size. Complicating things further, tuning varies from one brand to another. One of the notoriously variable notes is E♭ (third space), which is the second note in the bass line. The standard alto fingering of T/1O3/4OOO works on some bass instruments, while on others the fingering T/1O3/O56O is better.

14. Mary Had a Baby - *African-American spiritual*
(SA or ST; SB)

This Christmas song is heard with many different variations of both melody and text. The lyrics associated with this tune are simply *Mary had a baby, my Lord; Mary had a baby, my Lord; Mary had a baby, Mary had a baby, Mary had a baby, my Lord*. Subsequent verses include *What did she name him? Mary named him Jesus, Where was he born?* and *Born in a manger*. For singing, rhythms need to be adjusted to match the lyrics.

In this arrangement the harmony part includes some colorful altered harmonies that perk up what could be an otherwise rather ordinary song if given a standard "hymn" harmonization. The A♯s can be played with the same fingering as the B♭ (T/123/4O67 on alto; T/1O3/4OOO on tenor) in the final cadence, but I actually prefer to use the "trill" fingering for the A♯s (T/123/4O6O on alto; T/1O3/OOOO on tenor) because it is slightly higher in pitch and accentuates the upward harmonic inflection of the A♯s.

Like the E♭ in the bass part of Santiana (#13), the D♯ in measure 6 is inconsistent in tuning from one bass recorder to another. The standard alto fingering of T/1O3/4OOO works on some bass instruments, while on others the fingering T/1O3/O56O is better. Because the D♯ in "Mary Had a Baby" moves upward to an E, a fingering that is slightly sharper is probably best unless it is so sharp that it clashes with the B♮ in the melody. Those playing bass often need to experiment with different fingerings to find which one works best in a given situation.

I have simplified the rhythms in the bass part because of the instrument's slower response time.

15. Ma'oz Tzur - traditional Hanukkah song
(SA or ST)

The Hebrew poem "Ma'oz Tzur" (Rock of Ages) is believed to have been written in the 12th or 13th century CE. The tune given here was originally associated with the poem "Shene Zetim," but today it is almost exclusively sung as "Ma'oz Tzur." The melody probably originated as a German folk song in the 15th century.

The D♯ in measure 6 of the harmony part may be unfamiliar to some students. It was introduced for the first time in Part 5 of Volume 3 for soprano and Part 6 of Volume 3 for alto. The fingering itself is not overly difficult,[3] but when it is played on tenor several fingers must be placed simultaneously and precisely. When played on C recorders, the slurs in measure 12 of the melody and measure 19 of the harmony can be made smoother by using the trill fingering for B♮: T/O23/OOOO.

16. Freu' Dich des Lebens! (WoO 195) - canon in two parts
Ludwig van Beethoven (1770-1827)
(any combination of S and T)

The WoO designation on this piece stands for "without opus," and it is applied to any of Beethoven's works that were not published during his lifetime. He composed this little canon in 1825, writing just the melody with an indication of where the second voice should enter. I have provided it with a suitable ending that allows both voices to cadence together.

The E–F–E–F pattern in measures 2 and 3 of the top line and measures 4 and 5 of the bottom line is tricky whether played on soprano or tenor. The low Cs will be challenging for tenor players, particularly if the canon is played at a bright tempo as implied by its title: "Enjoy Life!"

17. Love's Content - Henry Lawes (1596-1662)
(SB, AB, or TB)

This ballad is found in *Select Ayres and Dialogues for One, Two, and Three Voyces; to the Theorbo-Lute or Basse-Viol*, published by John Playford in 1659. It is typical of the songwriting style of the 17th century: a single melody with an accompanying bass line that can be performed by a range of instruments. The theorbo was the bass member of the lute family, a plucked string instrument with a rounded back and about 14 strings tuned in pairs. The viol was a bowed string instrument that preceded and was eventually supplanted by the violin family.

---

3 C recorders – O/123/45ØO; F recorders – T/1O3/4OOO

The range of the melody lies very comfortably in the alto register. It requires partial-thumb fingerings for the high Fs and Gs. Musically speaking, I prefer the sound of alto for the melody in this piece. It is mellower and in the range of the human voice. If bass recorders are not available, or if the bass line is too difficult for the students, it may be played on a cello or rewritten up an octave in clefs suitable for viola or violin. On viola or violin, the pitch will be exactly that of the bass recorder, since the bass recorder sounds an octave higher than written.

Henry Lawes was an important and influential composer of the late English Renaissance. Little is known of his early life. He became a Gentleman of the Chapel Royal around 1626. He fell on hard times during the English Civil War (1642–1651) and greatly mourned the death of his younger brother William, also a respected composer. William had joined the royalist cause and was killed during the siege of Chester in 1645. With the restoration of the monarchy in 1660, Henry's position as court musician was restored. His anthem "Zadok the Priest" was sung at the coronation of King Charles II on April 23, 1661. Contemporary accounts indicate that he was severely ill at that time, and he died on October 21, 1662 of unknown causes. He was buried in the cloisters at Westminster Abbey. Henry composed over 430 songs as well as an assortment of hymns and psalm settings.

18. Ad Cantus Laetitiae - *anonymous, from Kloster Indersdorf (14th century)*
(SS, ST, AT, or TT)

"Ad Cantus Laetitiae" is a Latin Christmastide hymn from 14th-century Germany. The opening text translates to "To the song of joy, a child is born today. Rejoice!" The tempo of the music should be accordingly joyous. I have included here only the first and last sections of the hymn, the entire work being rather long and somewhat more repetitive than is manageable for many students.

The parallel perfect intervals that abound in this work are typical of medieval harmony. Composers did not shy away from harmonic clashes such as the major ninth and minor seventh that occur in measure 25, but they greatly preferred the open resonance of fifths and octaves, especially at cadences.

In performing this piece, take care that the top line is always higher in pitch than the lower line. The hymn was originally written for two tenor singers, and the lines should not cross. The indicated instrumentation options all accomplish this, but the hymn may also be performed with combined instruments playing the top line as long as there is a tenor recorder playing the bottom line. The top voice, when played on soprano or tenor, crosses into the partial-thumb register in several places. Use the partial-thumb setting for high E when preceded by a high F, and use the open thumb hole for high Es preceded by D or C. When the top voice is played on alto recorder all notes are in the closed-thumb register.

There are several low Fs, which could be difficult for students with small hands. The number of low Fs and Cs in the bottom line can make it difficult to play on tenor as well.

19. Te Solo Adoro (WoO 186) - canon in two parts
Ludwig van Beethoven (1770-1827)
(AT)

Although the top voice of this canon can be played on tenor recorder, it is much more manageable on alto. The A♭s in both voices require partial-hole fingerings: T/123/45ØO for alto and T/12O/45ØO for tenor. This is also the case for the E♭s in the tenor line: 123/45ØO. Students should note the similarity between these fingerings.

"Te Solo Adoro" was composed in 1823. It is a setting of the first stanza of a poem by Pietro Trapassi (1698–1782). The text, "Te solo adoro, mente infinita, fonte di vita, di verità" translates to "You alone I adore, infinite mind, source of life, of truth." The music should be slow and meditative.

The indication WoO stands for "without opus" and is used for compositions not published during the composer's lifetime. Beethoven did not give the canon first and second endings. A strict reading of the piece would result in the lower voice singing "Te" at the end without repeating. This making no musical or textual sense, the canon is often performed as I have arranged it, allowing the two lines to end together.

20. Cupid Detected - Henry Lawes (1596-1662)
(SB, AB, or TB)

Like "Love's Content" (17), "Cupid Detected" is found in Playford's *Select Ayres and Dialogues for One, Two, and Three Voyces; to the Theorbo-Lute or Basse-Viol.* It is typical of songs of the period, a single melodic line being accompanied by a bass instrument. See notes for #17 for details on accompanying instruments and Henry Lawes' life.

The bass part in "Cupid Detected" goes into the partial-thumb register twice, as does the melody when played on C recorders. When played on alto, the melody requires the use of finger 7 for the B♭s and low Fs. I prefer to hear the melody played on alto because its tone is mellower in this register. As in "Love's Content," the bass line may be performed on a cello or transposed up an octave and played on viola or violin (if violin is used, the final F must be played in the upper octave as shown in parentheses). There is a parenthetical ♮ above the B in measure 4. No natural is marked in Playford's edition, but to play a B♭ here would be out of keeping with the harmonic practices of Lawes' time. Be sure the students return to playing B♭ in measure 6.

21. Lachend Kommt der Sommer - canon in two parts
German folk song
(any combination of S, A, and T)

The German lyrics for this two part round are *Lachend, lachend, \ lachend, lachend \ kommt der Sommer \ über das Feld, \ über das– Feld kommt der \ Sommer, ha ha ha, \ lachend über das \ Feld*. A singable English translation is *Laughing, laughing, \ laughing, laughing \ comes the summer \ over the field, \ over the– field comes the \ summer, ha ha ha, \ laughing over the \ field*.

I have written the music in G Major so that it can be played easily on soprano, alto, or tenor instruments. On C recorders, the tune goes into the partial-thumb register, but the fingerings are relatively straightforward. The tune is most easily played on alto.

22. Dundai - canon in two parts - traditional Jewish dance tune
(any combination of S, A, and T)

"Dundai" can be danced as either a circle dance or a couples dance, so the tempo should be spirited but not too fast. I have written it here in G minor so that it can be played on both C and F recorders. On soprano and tenor it crosses the register break frequently, and this, together with the tricky fingerings for figures involving E♭s (e.g., measure 3), make it challenging to play. It is significantly easier to play on the alto.

23. La Adelita - Mexican folk song
(SA)

"La Adelita" is a corrido, a folk ballad originating in Mexico that follows a defined form and often addresses historical or social topics. Corridos typically have an instrumental introduction, which may also serve as an interlude between verses. The typical structure of a corrido is eight stanzas, each consisting of four to six lines of eight syllables. As in all folk traditions, there are many variations on the basic form of the corrido.

The song "La Adelita" originated during the Mexican Revolution. Although the woman named Adelita in the song is a fictional composite, the story is based on the real existence of women who joined the army, either fighting as soldiers or providing the fighters with medical care and food. The name Adelita soon came to be applied to any woman taking up a role in the Mexican military.

The A♯ in measure 26 of the alto part may be played with the trill fingering (T/123/4O5O). This is slightly sharper than the standard fingering for A♯/B♭ and heightens the upward harmonic inflection of the note.

24. Envoyons de l'avant - *French-Canadian voyageur song*
(any combination of S, A, and T)

The steady, rhythmic singing of voyageur songs helped fend off both mental and physical fatigue and coordinate the efforts of the paddlers. The numerous C♯s and F♯s make "Envoyens de l'avant" harder to play on alto than on C recorders.

The fingering for D♯ (measure 5) on C recorders (O/O23/456O) was introduced in Vol. 3 Part 4, but may still be unfamiliar. It is the same fingering that is used for the E♭ on the fourth space. The fingering for this note on alto recorder is T/1O3/4OOO.

25. Dry Those Eyes - *from The Ariels Songs in the Play call'd The Tempest - John Banister (1630-1679)*
(SA or SB; TB)

The history of English theater from Shakespeare's time until the middle of the 17th century is one of creative brilliance and continuous challenge. Playwrights were obliged to cater to the whims of nobility and aristocracy; many troupes traveled the countryside performing for whatever they could earn; and periodic outbreaks of plague resulted in the closing of theaters and other public venues. Then, in 1640, the Puritan faction took control of Parliament, and by 1642 all theaters in London were shut down. This was the state of things until 1660, when the monarchy was restored.

John Banister was of the new generation of English musicians writing music in a new style which had developed on the continent: a style known today as the baroque. His talent was such that it attracted the attention of King Charles II, who sent him to France for further training. When Banister returned to England he was made leader of the king's own band. In 1676 Banister composed music to accompany a performance of Shakespeare's *The Tempest*. "Dry Those Eyes" is one of these songs. The singer on stage would probably have been accompanied by a lutenist, perhaps with the addition of a bass viol. Unlike today, musicians were typically seated to the side of the stage, in a balcony, or perhaps in the tiring house.[4] They were often in full view of the audience.

The high F♮ in measure 9 of the soprano part uses the partial-hole setting of the thumb, and the finger changes between E♭ and F♮ are tricky. If the melody is played on tenor, the bass line must be played on bass recorder. The alto/tenor version of the bass line can be used only when the melody is played on soprano. If lower recorders are not available to play the bass line, it may be played on a cello.

---

4 A tiring house was a section of the theater reserved for actors and used for costume changes and awaiting entrance cues.

26. *Le Berger Fidèle* - Louise Farrenc (1804-1875)
(SS, ST, AT, or TT)

Louise Farrenc, née Dumont, was a French virtuoso pianist and composer who, in her musical career, faced many challenges simply because of her gender. As a child, she showed considerable talent as a pianist and composer, and she was accepted at the age of fifteen as a composition student by Anton Reicha, a friend of Beethoven who considerably influenced many of the most prominent composers of the time. However, since the Paris Conservatory did not permit women to take composition classes, she had to take private lessons with Reicha.

At the age of seventeen, she married flutist Aristide Farrenc and began touring France with him, performing as a flute and piano duo. Eventually Aristide tired of concertizing[5] and they returned to Paris where they founded a music publishing firm. Together they compiled and published 20 volumes of the *Trésor des pianistes*, which featured works by important early keyboard composers.[6] Louise resumed her studies with Reicha and continued to perform concerts as a solo pianist. By 1842, she had become so widely recognized as a virtuoso pianist that she was offered a position as Professor of Piano at the Paris Conservatory. She was the only woman to hold this position in the entire 19th century. She was highly successful as a teacher, yet for years she was paid less than the male teachers at the conservatory. She began composing extensively, producing three symphonies, several chamber works, and dozens of works for solo piano. It was only the brilliant success of her Nonet for winds and strings, Op. 38, that enabled her to finally demand and receive equal pay. Louise Farrenc was awarded the Prix Chartier by the French Academy of Fine Arts in 1861 and 1869.[7]

Many of Farrenc's compositions were large-scale pieces: symphonies, concert overtures, and variations for orchestra, virtuosic piano solos, and lengthy chamber works. In this context, "Le Berger Fidèle" stands out as an anomaly: a short, delicate song for voice and guitar. Despite its apparent simplicity, though, the music displays a deft and subtle hand when it comes to harmony and voicing.

I have transposed the music from A Major to D Major so that the melody can be played on C recorders or on alto. The accompaniment line (S/T) must remain below the range of melody. It should be played on soprano only if the melody is

---

[5] In those days, most touring musicians had to do much more than perform. They took care of bookings, promotion, sales, transportation, housing and everything else.

[6] Louise and Aristide collaborated on the first eight volumes. After Aristide's death in 1865, Louise continued the project, publishing another twelve volumes by 1872.

[7] The Prix Chartier was an award given for outstanding chamber music composition by the Academy of Fine Arts. It was awarded almost every year from 1861 to 1942. Louise Farrenc was the second person to receive this prize, and one of only three women ever. She was also one of the few composers to be given the award more than once.

played exclusively on soprano. Both melody and accompaniment are difficult. The melody frequently moves by wide intervals, which must nevertheless be smooth and vocal in sound. The rolling arpeggios of the accompaniment must be steady and sound relaxed despite fingering difficulties (especially the low C♯s when played on tenor). The E♯ in measure 7 of the accompaniment can be played with the trill fingering for F♮: T/123/4O5O. This allows finger 7 to lift rather than slip to the side when moving from C♯ to E♯.

PART B - Music in Three Parts

Many of the pieces in this section have alternative instrumentations, allowing them to be played with or without bass. Many also sound quite satisfactory with two voices, usually soprano and alto. Several of the pieces toward the end of this section are quite difficult.

27. Te Aroha - Māori folk song, Aotearoa (New Zealand)
(SAB or SAT; SA)

"Te Aroha" is a Māori song about love, hope, and peace. Aotearoa is the Māori name for New Zealand. Te Aroha is also the name of a small town on the North Island. While I have generally avoided writing harmonies for indigenous melodies, many Māori songs are performed by indigenous singers with harmonies in the style of European tonality. This arrangement uses a technique called "layering," in which the melody begins alone and additional voices are added on repetitions.

The tenor and bass parts are identical, so the piece sounds the same whether played with SAT or SAB. The third voice is actually easier to play on bass recorder than on tenor, since it uses only fingers from the left (top) hand. The piece can be performed with both tenor and bass instruments as long as the third voice does not overpower the other two.

"Te Aroha" can also be performed with tenor recorders playing the top line. This puts the harmony below the melody, but does not result in any awkward harmonic inversions. In some ways, playing the piece with TAT or TAB is more satisfying because of the deeper, richer timbre of the tenor instrument. However, this could leave students who play only soprano recorder with nothing to do. It is admissible to play "Te Aroha" with both soprano and tenor recorders on the top line, again with the caveat that the alto part, which carries the melody, must not be overpowered.

This arrangement can also be performed with just the top two voices, though the third voice adds harmonic richness.

28. Mama Paquita - Brazilian folk song
(SAT or SAB; AT or AB; SA)

In this arrangement the melody is heard in the alto line while the soprano and tenor/bass parts add a rhythmic accompaniment. The tenor and bass parts are identical, and either or both may be used. Just make sure the accompaniment does not overpower the melody. While the three voice harmonization is preferred, the piece can be performed with the alto melody accompanied by just one of the other voices. Played with sopranos and altos only, there are gaps between the phrases, so performance with AT or AB is preferable. Alternatively, soprano players can be divided between the soprano and tenor lines, though the between-phrase patterns will be an octave higher than when played on the tenor.

29. Askari eee - Tanzanian folk song
(SAT or SAB)

This setting of "Askari eee" uses two techniques often found in music from sub-Saharan Africa. The first is layering; the song starts with all voices playing the melody, then in the third section the soprano and alto lines split off into harmony. The second is the use of parallel triads ubiquitous to vocal music of this region.

The tenor and bass lines are displaced by an octave, but otherwise identical. The piece can be played with either or both. Using both instruments augments the parallel texture of the voicing. The bass and tenor parts use only three notes, all in a comfortable register, making this piece useful for introducing students to the larger instruments.

30. Chevaliers de la Table Ronde - French folk song
(SAT or SAB; SA; ST or SB)

It might seem surprising that the French would be interested in the tales of King Arthur, but Brittany was settled in the 4th century by Bretons moving south from what are now the areas of Devon and Cornwall, and there are two islands off the coast of Brittany have been cited as the possible inspiration for the isle of Avalon. In addition, it was the French duchess and English queen Eleanor of Aquitaine (c. 1124–1204) who promoted the legends as models of courtly behavior.[8]

---

[8] Those who use the Arthurian romances as teaching material should bear in mind that they are by no means an accurate representation of medieval life or society. The sparse legendary material recorded in the ninth century Historia Britonum was expanded in the twelfth century by Geoffrey of Monmouth and then heavily romanticized by Chretien de Troyas and Thomas Malory.

The tenor and bass parts in this setting are identical, and the piece may be played with either or both instruments as long as balance is maintained. The relative simplicity of the third voice makes "Chevaliers de la Table Ronde" an excellent choice for introducing students to the larger tenor and bass instruments. It also sounds fine played with just the soprano and alto parts. It is possible that students learning this piece might not have previously encountered changes of meter. In the second half of "Chevaliers de la Table Ronde," the changes between 3/4 and 2/4 time will require that they remain alert. The speed of the quarter note remains constant.

31. Sine Nomine - Ralph Vaughan Williams (1872-1958)
(SAT or SAB)

Ralph (pronounced "Rafe") Vaughan Williams' familiar hymn is sung to many different lyrics, both religious and secular. It is commonly known by the first line of the most familiar text, "For all the saints."

The tenor and bass parts in this arrangement are identical, and the piece may be played with either or both instruments, bearing in mind that the three voices must be in balance. In the absence of tenor or bass, the setting sounds satisfactory played with just soprano and alto, though there are some open fourths that sound harmonically incomplete.

The tenor and bass parts have a fairly wide range that pushes the tenor to its lowest note and the bass into the partial thumb register. Overall, the tenor part is easier.

32. Roll the Old Chariot Along - Capstan shanty
(SAT or SAB; SA; ST or SB)

Sea shanties are maritime work songs, usually with a specific purpose. "Roll the Old Chariot Along" is a capstan shanty. A capstan was a large vertical winch into which long wooden bars could be inserted. The crew would walk in circles pushing these bars to turn the capstan and thereby raise the ship's anchor or hoist heavy loads. The shantyman would often stand atop the center of the capstan singing the shanty or playing it on a fiddle or tin whistle. A steady tempo was necessary to keep the crew all pushing at the same speed.

The tenor and bass parts in this setting are identical. Either or both instruments may be used, making sure that balance between the voices is maintained. With only four pitches being used by tenor and bass, "Roll the Old Chariot Along" is an excellent piece for students just beginning to play these larger instruments. The bass part is particularly useful because it uses top hand fingerings only. The tenor part does reach low C, but there is time to find finger 7 during the preceding rest.

As with any shanty, the number and nature of the verses varies. A few of the most common lyrics are below:

Oh, a \ drop of Nelson's \ blood wouldn't \ do us any \ harm, (3 times)
And we'll \ all hang \ on be-\hind.

(refrain) *So we'll \ ro-o-\oll the old \ chariot a-\long,*
And we'll \ ro-o-\oll the old \ chariot a-\long,
So we'll \ ro-o-oll the old \ chariot a-\long,
And we'll \ all hang \ on be-\hind.

Oh, a plate of Irish stew wouldn't do us any harm, (3 times)
And we'll all hang on behind.

(refrain)

Oh a nice watch below wouldn't do us any harm, (3 times)
And we'll all hang on behind.

(refrain)

Oh, we'd be alright if the wind was in our sails, (3 times)
And we'll all hang on behind.

(refrain)

Other verses might refer to "a nice fat cook," "a night upon the shore," "a night on the town." Needless to say, there are often verses with implicit or explicit sexual lyrics that are not suitable for use with young students.

"A drop of Nelson's blood" is a reference to the preservation of Admiral Lord Nelson's body in brandy after his death in the Battle of Trafalgar. The inclusion of camphor and myrrh in the preservative would, of course, have rendered the brandy undrinkable.

33. Julia, Julia, Pela la Yuca - Panamanian folk song
(SAT)

In this arrangement the melody is distributed among the three parts, so none can be omitted. The range of each part is fairly narrow and stays in the most comfortable register for all instruments.

The rhythmic pattern of beats 1 and 2 of every measure is characteristic of much Latin music, but unusual to those more familiar with English and U.S. folk music. The eight sixteenth-note subdivisions in these two beats are grouped as 3-3-2 rather than the more straightforward 4-4. The result is that each measure feels like it includes three short beats of unequal length followed by two equal quarter-note beats. This rhythmic pattern is called a *cinquillo*, and it is found in much Caribbean and Latin American music. It originated in sub-Saharan Africa and came to the Americas with African captives of the slave trade. When a cinquillo is followed by four unsyncopated eighth notes, as it is heard in the melody, it is known as a *baqueteo*.

34. Round and Round the Earth Is Turning
anonymous round in three parts
(any combination of S, A, and T, with optional B)

This three-part round is in the dorian mode, a minor key with the sixth scale degree raised (rather than lowered as in the standard "natural minor" or aeolian mode). The dorian mode is very common in European folk music traditions. It is a particularly interesting mode in that the two tetrachords (in this case A–B–C–D and E–F♯–G–A) are identical with each other and also with their inversions, each consisting of a whole step, a half step, and a whole step.

The bass part doubles the third voice an octave lower. The round can be played with single instrumentation on each line (for example, SAT or ATB) or with combinations of instruments for any voice. I have written the bass part to double the third voice only because the bass recorder requires significantly more lung capacity than the others. In reality, basses can play along with any of the three voices if so desired.

As written, the melody lies most comfortably on F recorders. Played on C recorders, it crosses the register break in the third and fourth measures, requiring the use of the partial-hole setting of the thumb.

The lyrics are: (1) *Round and round the \ Earth– is turning,* \ (2) *Turning always \ in–to morning,* \ (3) *And from morning \ in–to night.*

35. Red Iron Ore - U.S. folk song
(SAT; SA)

"Red Iron Ore" tells the story of a sailor working on an ore ship in the Great Lakes. Iron ore is a major product in the upper Midwest, and the Great Lakes long provided the best means of transporting ore from the mines in the north to the larger cities in the southern part of the region.

The lyrics of the first verse are:
Come \ all ye bold sailors who \ follow the lakes,
On an \ iron ore vessel your \ living to make,
*I \ shipped in Chicago, bid a-\dieu to the shore, *
bound a-\way to Escanaba for \ red iron ore.
Derry \ down, down, \ down, derry down.

Escabana is a port city on the Upper Peninsula of Michigan, located on the west side of Little Bay de Noc, one of the region's many bays. Escabana has a deep harbor, making it an ideal port for shipping. The city takes its name from the Escabana River which flows into Little Bay de Noc. The river's name is from the Algonquin word meaning "land of the red buck." The name of Little Bay de Noc is derived from the name of the Noquet, an indigenous tribe whose traditional homeland lay along the shores of this and other bays in the area. In later verses of the song, it becomes clear that Escabana is also the name of the tugboat that pulled the ore ships out of the harbor.

The low F♯s in the alto part may be challenging for students with small hands. The low D♯s in the tenor part are all neighbored by low Es, and are therefore not hard to manage. The most challenging aspect of this piece is probably the fermatas in measures 5, 6, and 9. All players must end the held note together and then, after a breath, begin the next phrase together.

The tune is noticeably similar to the well known ballad, "Sweet Betsy from Pike," which was itself derived from an earlier ballad called "Villikins and His Dinah," first published in 1853. "Villikins" in turn is a parody of "William and Dinah," a traditional song dating to earlier in the 19th century. Another similar tune is "Down, Down, Down" (#85). This kind of musical borrowing is very common in folk music traditions. It can be difficult to trace influences. However, since Escabana was established as a port town in 1863 and "Sweet Betsy from Pike" was first published in 1858, if there is any repurposing of melodies, it is clear that "Red Iron Ore" would have been derivative.

36. Alla Matina (Bella Ciao) - *Italian folk song*
(SAT or SAB)

This song originated in northern Italy, where it was sung by workers in the rice paddies to protest the extreme difficulties of their labor. The paddies were flooded for several weeks in the spring, and during this time required constant weeding and cultivation. It was back-breaking work, and the workers—mostly women—had to contend with biting insects, squelching mud, and harsh supervision. The song makes reference to the supervisor "standing with his staff," implying that those who did not work hard enough would be beaten.

Shortly after the end of WWII, the tune, with new lyrics and known as "Bella Ciao" (good-bye, beautiful one), became associated with the Italian partisan movement. Partisans were Italian groups, both military and civilian, that resisted the Nazi invasion and the dictatorial fascist rule of Benito Mussolini. The partisans were of wide-ranging ideologies and included socialists, communists, anarchists, democrats, republicans,[9] labor leaders, Protestants, Catholics, and those who simply wanted to rid Italy of dictatorial and foreign rulers. It was an alliance of convenience, and when Italian fascism fell in 1945, the various partisan factions began contending with each other. Eventually, *Bella Ciao* came to be associated with Italian communists, even though it had been sung by diverse political and social parties.

"Bella Ciao" is sometimes sung or played in the style of a military march, but I have chosen to give it a more contemplative, almost melancholy, character that reflects its origins. Both melody and accompaniment should be played smoothly. This will be difficult in places where the line crosses the register break (measure 7 in the soprano and bass parts) and where G♯s appear in the tenor and bass parts.

37. Cielito Lindo - *Quirino Mendoza y Cortés (1862-1957)*
(SAB or STB; SA or ST)

Quirino Mendoza y Cortés was a prominent Mexican composer who, in 1882, wrote the classic song "Cielito Lindo," which became a standard among Mariachi bands. He was a primary school music teacher for several decades and also served as the director of the military orchestra during the Mexican Revolution. "Cielito Lindo" translates literally as "pretty little sky" and is a term of endearment; the song is a love ballad. That said, one would not be remiss in using the music in conjunction with a study of weather phenomena.

In this setting, the melody is shared by the treble voices. The middle part can be played on alto or tenor, though alto is preferred, since the tenor crosses the register break in several places. The bass part, while providing textural and harmonic richness, is easily omitted.

The rhythmic configuration of "Cielito Lindo" is one with which students may be unfamiliar, but which is ubiquitous to much Mexican folk music: the hemiola. A hemiola is the replacement of two three-beat figures (here two measures of 3/4 time) by three two-beat figures. It creates the effect of changing meters. The association of hemiolas with Latin music is so strong that composer Leonard

---

[9] The terms "democrat" and "republican" in this context have nothing to do with American political parties, but rather indicate those who promoted the idea of a democracy (governance by the populace) or a republic (governance by elected representatives of the populace).

Bernstein used it to evoke a Puerto Rican flavor in the song "America" from *West Side Story*. The juxtaposition of a hemiola in the bass against two 3/4 bars in the upper voices In measures 13 and 14 may be challenging.

38. Au Chant de l'alouette - French-Canadian voyageur song
(SAT or SAB; SA)

"Au Chant de l'alouette" is a call-and-response song about a girl talking to a songbird while picking berries. The call-and-response character can be achieved by playing the top line as a solo the first time each section is played, this being echoed by the other players.

With the exception of the C in measure 3, the tenor and bass parts in this arrangement are identical. I displaced the C in the tenor so that tenor players would not need to use finger 7 at all to play the piece. Frequent B♭s in the soprano line and B♭s and E♭s in the alto line will require some finger dexterity. The dotted rhythms in the soprano part may tend to slow down the music's pulse. This can be avoided by playing the dotted eighth note as a light staccato, almost like an eighth note followed by a sixteenth rest. As with any work song, the beat must be steady.

39. Pastyme with Good Companye (The Kynges Balade)
King Henry VIII of England
(SAB or STB; SA or ST; SB)

As the younger son of King Henry VII, Henry Tudor was not expected to reign as king. Then, in 1502 when Henry was ten years old, the royal heir, Arthur, died, and Henry became first in line to the throne. Henry became king in 1509 at the age of 17.

Henry's education, like that of any royal youth, included a strong arts component, and he demonstrated considerable talent as a musician, composing several songs. "Pastyme with Good Companye" was written when Henry was in his early twenties or perhaps in his teens. It was first published around 1513. The song celebrates and seeks to justify the extravagant lifestyle of medieval aristocracy. Henry asserts that he will "hunt, sing, and dance" his entire life, because "idleness is chief mistress of vices all."

With its snappy dotted rhythms and simple four-bar structure, "Pastyme with Good Companye" soon became popular among commoners as well as at court. However, the pastimes of the former group would not have included hunting, which was a matter of necessity rather than sport and limited to trapping small animals and birds. Deer and other large game belonged to the king, and penalties for poaching could be quite severe.

The voicing in this arrangement is as it appears in the c. 1513 manuscript. I have raised cadential F♮s to F♯ and lowered the E♮s in the bass line to E♭ in keeping with standard practice. Soprano players will need to observe the accidentals carefully. The large number of F♮s and B♭s in the treble clef parts make for some tricky finger changes. So do the E♭s and B♭s in the bass part.

40. Ma Nishtana - *traditional Passover song*
(SAT or SAB; SA)

In this arrangement the melody begins in the soprano part and shifts to the alto at the upbeat to measure 13. The alto part extends into the partial-thumb register and is more difficult to play than the other parts. The tenor and bass parts are identical. Either or both instruments may be used. The finger changes between F♯ and D♯ in the tenor and bass parts are tricky and may require some focused practice. The piece also sounds good with only soprano and alto instruments playing the top two lines.

41. Dayenu - *traditional Passover song*
(SAT; SA)

I arranged this Passover song for just treble clef recorders in order to maintain the jubilant spirit of the tune. The jumps in measure 3 of the soprano part are tricky and hard to play cleanly. The C♯s in the alto part are likewise challenging. This arrangement can be played with only the soprano and alto parts, but the interesting harmonic coloring in measure 3 and the lively descending "dayenu" in the first ending will be lost.

42. Country Gardens - *English Morris tune*
(SAB or SAT; SA; ST or SB)

Dating as far back as the early 18th century, "Country Gardens" was popularized when American composer Percy Grainger arranged it for solo piano. It has remained a mainstay of educational music literature ever since. This arrangement is loosely based on Grainger's version.

The chromaticism in the alto part is not overly difficult if the students have learned the necessary fingerings, but it will keep them alert. The dotted rhythms in the soprano part must not be permitted to slow the tempo. Playing the dotted eighth note short and light, as though the it were written as an eighth note followed by a sixteenth rest and a sixteenth note, will help keep the rhythm lively and the tempo from dragging.

This setting can be played with just the soprano and alto parts, though the third voice adds a dance-like bounce. The tenor and bass parts are identical with the exception of a few octave displacements that do not affect the voicing. The piece can also be played with just the soprano and tenor/bass parts, but this loses the chromatic interest of the alto part. Overall, the three-part instrumentation is preferred.

43. Star in the East - Shape note hymn from Southern Harmony and Musical Companion (1854)
(mixed SAT with Bass)

Shape note is a method of musical notation that was devised in late 18th-century England. It quickly became prominent in singing schools in America, where it was introduced in *The Easy Instructor* of 1801. The method involves using note heads of various shapes which indicate the position and function of each note in the musical scale. The idea was that if a music student knew the sound of the scale, they would be better able to read music using shape notes. Controlled studies have confirmed this to be the case.

In the US, shape note hymns were written for singing schools and social singing throughout the eighteenth and nineteenth centuries. Although the method has largely been abandoned in favor of standard notation, many of the hymns remain in church repertoire.

As a musical style, shape note favored open fifths and parallel voicing. These characteristics are readily apparent in the Christmas hymn "Star in the East." The harmonies will perplex students whose ears have become accustomed to music of European composers of the time. There are passing dissonances which are not resolved according to the "rules" of tonal harmony. There are also parallel fifths and inverted harmonies that were to be avoided according to the same precedents.

Another feature of shape note songs is that the parts were not designated by vocal type. Singers would sing whichever part they chose in the range that was comfortable to them. This typically resulted in each musical line being doubled at the octave, creating a thick, rich texture unlike that of any other musical style of the time. I have sought to imitate this here by arranging the upper and middle voices in such a way that they can be performed by soprano/alto and soprano/tenor respectively. It is not necessary to double voices, however. The bass part is essential to the harmonies and should not be omitted.

44. Ulele - Congolese folk song
(any combination of S, A, and T, with optional B)

This song was transcribed from a live recording of Congolese singers. The setting exhibits two characteristics ubiquitous to central African music: layering and parallel voicing. The first six measures are in unison. In the next six, the middle voice splits off into an exclamatory response while the others continue with the initial material. In the final six measures, the top voice splits off into parallel harmonization. Each of the three voices may be played on any of the treble clef recorders, and bass recorder may be used for the bottom voice, which plays the initial theme throughout. Given the range of notes, the top and middle voices are most easily played on alto recorders, while the third voice is equally easy on any instrument.

45. Aylesbury
from The New-Brunswick Collection of Sacred Music (1818)
(combinations of S, A, and T, with optional B)

This hymn may be played with soprano, alto, and/or tenor on the top two voices, and with soprano, tenor, and/or bass on the third voice. To capture the effect of shape note singing, it is preferable to play each of the three voices with an assortment of instruments playing in octaves. See the notes for "Star in the East" (#43) for more information on shape note songs.

The top two lines are more easily played on alto than on C recorders. The middle voice crosses the register break on C instruments, but is in the lower register for alto. The unusual voicing and varied phrase lengths give the hymn a character reminiscent of medieval music.

46. Blow Thy Horne, Hunter - William Cornysh (1465-1523)
(SAB or STB; SA or ST)

William Cornysh (also spelled Cornish and Cornyshe) was a composer, poet, and actor of the English Renaissance and a favorite of King Henry VIII. He composed a large number of songs and madrigals, both sacred and secular, as well as motets, masses, and other religious choral music. The madrigal "Blow Thy Horne, Hunter" is from a song book once owned by Henry, known simply as *The Henry VIII Manuscript*.

The middle voice can be played on either alto or tenor recorder, but is best suited to the alto. Those playing bass must be particularly attentive to the rhythm in measure 8. Up to that point the voices are largely homophonic. Then, suddenly, the bass part moves two beats before the others. The meter change at the end is not especially difficult; the half note remains constant throughout the entire piece.

47. Cape Cod Girls - Capstan shanty
(SAT or SAB; SA; ST or SB)

Cape Cod and the nearby islands of Nantucket and Martha's Vineyard figured prominently in the whaling industry of the eighteenth and nineteenth centuries. Also known as "Cape Cod Boys," this sea song has a variety of humorous verses:

Cape Cod girls, they \ have no combs, Heave a-\way, heave a-\way! They \ comb their hair with \ codfish bones, We are \ bound for Aus-\tralia.

(refrain) *Heave away, my \ bonny, bonny boys, Heave a-\way, Heave a-\way! \ Heave away, and \ don't you make a noise, We are\ bound for Aus-\tralia.*

Other verses include *Cape Cod Boys, they have no sleds, they ride down hills on codfish heads*; *Cape Cod doctors have no pills, they give their patients codfish gills*; and *Cape Cod sailors have no sails, they rig their ships with codfish tails*. My students have always enjoyed making their own whimsical verses as well.

The soprano part crosses the register break in the refrain, but otherwise "Cape Cod Girls" is relatively easy to play. Students always enjoy the way the harmony voices imitate the melody on "heave away." See "Santiana" (#13) and "Roll the Old Chariot Along" (#32) for information on capstans and capstan shanties.

48. All Joy to Great Caesar
from Playford's Apollo's Banquet (1687)
(SAT, SST, SAB or SSB; SA or SS)

Students who play the violin may recognize this tune as "La Folia," which Arcangelo Corelli used in his violin sonata, Op. 5 No. 12, commonly known as the *La Folia Variations* and first published in 1700. La Folia is an ancient tune that originated not as a melody, but rather as a harmonic sequence over which a number of melodies could be composed. At least two versions of the melody predate Corelli's: the 1685 publication of Playford's *The Division Violin*, in which it is referred to as "Faronell's Division on a Ground,"[10] and in the 1687 publication of Playford's *Apollo's Banquet* as a country dance tune with the rather lengthy and enigmatic title "The tune of Farrinel's Ground, to the song of (All Joy to Great Caesar)." The first four measures of the tune were also used in *The Beggar's Opera* (1728). According to British musicologist Edward J. Dent (1876–1957),

---

10 A "division" in the Baroque era was a variation or set of variations of a tune. A "ground" was a repeating bass line.

"Joy to Great Caesar" is a fragment of the famous Follia traceable to a Portuguese origin in the 17th century, known in England as Farinel's Ground (c. 1690) from its arranger Michel Farinel, a Frenchman. It was used by John Blow in a Birthday Ode for James II (hence the words "Great Caesar").[11]

In addition, Royalist and anti-Catholic writer Thomas D'Urfey (c. 1653–1723) used Farrinel's Ground as a basis for the propaganda song "Joy to Great Caesar" praising King Charles II of England and criticizing the Pope.

Apart from performing Corelli's sonata, my initial foray into this tune was in the 1980s when I realized that with slight modification it could be played on soprano recorders as a canon with the second voice starting a fifth lower than the first. I later adapted the second voice to be playable on alto and added a bass line for tenor or bass recorder that is modeled on Corelli's.

The second canonic voice is easier to play on alto than on soprano. The third voice is more approachable on tenor than on bass; played on bass it crosses the register break several times and has some awkward fingerings. The canonic voices can be played without the bass line.

49. Jefferson and Liberty - U.S. folk song
(SAT or SAB)

American political campaigns have long used music to persuade voters, and "Jefferson and Liberty," using an old Irish jig called "Gobby-O," was one of the first.[12]

(verse) The– \ gloomy night– be-\fore us lies, The \ reign– of terror– \ now– is o'er–; Its \ gags, inqui-si-\tors and spies, Its \ hordes– of harpies– \ are no more. (refrain) Re-\joice, Columbia's \ sons, rejoice, To \ tyrants never \ bend– the knee, But \ join with heart and \ soul– and voice For \ Je–fferson and \ Liberty.

There are many verses, each laden with more anti-monarchist rhetoric than the last. There is considerable irony, of course, in Jefferson, an enslaver, campaigning on the idea of liberty. One can only assume that "liberty" referred to political

---

11 *The Beggar's Opera, written by John Gay, The Overture and the Songs Composed by John Christopher Pepusch (vocal score)* Edited by Edward J. Dent, London, Oxford University Press, 1954.

12 The purported earliest was "Adams and Liberty," which was sung to the popular British drinking song "To Anacreon in Heaven." And yes, that is the same tune which was later attached to Francis Scott Key's poem "The Defense of Fort McHenry" to become "The Star Spangled Banner."

independence, not to individual freedom. Contrary to the once popular notion, Jefferson did not free his slaves. He released only two during his lifetime, and another five in his will, but at his the time of his death Jefferson was so heavily in debt that his heirs sold 130 slaves to pay his creditors. Jefferson's views on slavery seem to have been inconsistent at best, as he supported the prohibition of slavery in the western territories and yet opposed general emancipation, claiming that it would lead to conflict between white people and former slaves.

The melody in this arrangement of "Jefferson and Liberty" begins in the soprano part and moves to the alto part at the midpoint. In the first half, the accompaniment should be articulate and light. Be careful that playing staccato does not result in the release of too much air. Breaths should be taken only when needed, not during every rest. The tenor and bass parts are harmonically identical, though often an octave apart. Students playing bass will need to adjust for the instrument's slow response time, especially on the lowest notes.

50. We Shall Overcome - Gospel hymn
(SAT or SAB; SA)

This well-known Gospel song became emblematic of the American civil rights movement of the 1960s. The melody seems to derive from a much older song, known both as "No More Slavery Chains for Me" and "Many Thousands Gone," which was a favorite of the Black English composer Samuel Coleridge-Taylor (composer of "Andalla," #118; and "St Agnes Eve," #126). Coleridge-Taylor published an arrangement of "Many Thousands Gone" in his *24 Negro Melodies*, Op. 59. The familiar lyrics are an adaptation of "I'll Overcome Some Day," by Rev. Charles Albert Tindley (1851–1933).

This arrangement is fairly straightforward and can be played in three parts (SAT or SAB) or two (SA). The alto and tenor parts require the use of finger 7 and may be difficult for students with smaller hands. The tenor and bass parts are identical except for a couple of octave displacements.

51. Gathering Peascods - English round dance tune
from Playford's The English Dancing Master[13] (1651)
(SAT or SAB; SA)

"Gathering Peascods" was a popular dance of the mid-17th century. It was danced in a ring with any number of couples. As was standard practice, Playford published only the melody. Harmony and embellishments would have been added by the musicians.

---

13 The first edition (1651) of Playford's collection of dance music was called *The English Dancing Master*. Subsequent editions dropped the word "English."

The tenor and bass lines in this setting are identical except for the octave displacement of two notes in the second section. The two low C♮s in the tenor part and the low F♯ in the alto may be difficult for students with smaller hands.

For those who are interested, Playford's instructions for the dance can be found online at https://playforddances.com/dances/gathering-peascods/

52. Kum Bachur Atzel - anonymous Hebrew round in three parts
(any combination of S, A, and T)

"Get up, lazy fellow, the rooster is crowing!" This bright round is excellent for waking up sleepy middle schoolers in the morning. As written here, it is playable on any treble clef recorder. Quick alternations between A and B♭ in the second phrase require finger dexterity, and the low F♮s may be difficult for some students to play on alto and tenor instruments, but otherwise the music is pretty straightforward.

53. Yankee Doodle - U.S. folk song
(SAT or SAB; SA)

According to the Library of Congress archives, "Yankee Doodle" predates the American Revolution. Some sources attribute the song to a British army surgeon who, during the French and Indian Wars, was mocking the colonial soldiers' incompetence. The origin of the word "Yankee" is uncertain and debated, but in 18th century British parlance a "doodle" was a fool. A "dandy" was a man who dressed foppishly and had affected manners. Essentially, the term "Yankee Doodle Dandy" meant "foolish, pretentious American."

During the American Civil War, soldiers of the Confederacy would parody the song, singing, "Yankee Doodle had a mind to whip the southern traitors, because they did not choose to live on codfish and potatoes." Subsequent verses accused the Yankees of cowardice and of trying to steal the southerners' slaves[14] because that was the only way they would be able to win the war. There are references to the Confederate victory at Bull Run, and northerners are repeatedly called thieves, drunkards, and meddlers.

This arrangement uses drones in imitation of the sound of bagpipes. There is no evidence that bagpipes were used for marching by the Continental Army, and none that any self respecting 18th-century Highlander would have played a British tune on pipes, but it's a good sound and it works well for the piece. The quarter note pattern at the beginning of the tenor/bass part is intended to evoke marching and should be played deliberately and steadily. The third voice reaches low C, which is difficult on tenor.

---

14 The parody used a common racial slur rather than "slaves."

54. The British Grenadiers - English folk song
(SAT; SAB; SA; ST; or SB)

The origins of this well known English march are obscure. A similar melody, "The New Bath," was printed in the 1686 printing of Playford's *The Dancing Master*, albeit in 6/4 time. It also is remarkably similar to a number of other traditional dance tunes. Because of this, "The British Grenadiers" is sometimes cited as a prime example of the folk process.

The soprano and alto lines are not difficult to play, and the arrangement works quite well when played with only these two parts. The third voice reaches low C when played on tenor and goes above the register break when played on bass and is therefore harder to play.

One of my eighth-grade classes had fun playing the soprano lines of "The British Grenadiers" and "Yankee Doodle" simultaneously. The meter and structure are the same, but the harmonic implications of the tunes are different. The resulting clashes (parallel sevenths!) made it difficult for each group to hold on to their own tune and also gave the impression of a musical battle. (I cannot claim to have come up with this idea on my own; several composers in the Baroque era wrote musical depictions of battles using music in different keys and even different meters played together.)

55. We'll Rant and We'll Roar (The Ryans and the Pittmans)
Newfoundland folk song
(SAT or SAB; SA)

Although Newfoundland (pronounced "noo´-fuhn-land") is the source of many marvelous sea songs, this one is derived from the British shanty "Spanish Ladies." The gist of the song is that a Newfoundland sailor named Bob Pittman is determined to marry "sweet Biddy" as soon as he can save up enough money "for a ring and the priest, a couple of dollars for clean shirts and collars, and a handful of coppers to make up a feast." His dilemma is that there are a number of other women in various ports with whom he has been galavanting, and from the sound of things he burns through his wages so fast that he is unlikely to be able to "plank the cash down" any time soon. The alternate title of "The Ryans and the Pittmans" is an enigma, since no one named Ryan is mentioned anywhere in the song.

The tenor and bass parts in this arrangement jump quite a bit and are more difficult than the soprano and alto parts. There are also places with quickly changing chromatics. If these lines are too difficult, or if tenor and bass instruments are not available, the music sounds perfectly fine with just soprano and alto. I have introduced a key change in this arrangement, both to put the melody more comfortably in the alto range for the second strain, and also to introduce students to the idea of changing keys. The quick transition from G Major to C Major requires that soprano players quickly adjust to playing F♮s. Although the third strain returns to G Major, there are minor changes in the harmony parts. Students playing those lines must stay alert and not play by ear. Those playing tenor or bass in this piece must remain alert; there are a few places with quick chromatic changes.

56. Ah Robin, Gentle Robin - William Cornysh (1465-1523)
(S and/or T Pes with A melody)

In his madrigal "Ah Robin, Gentle Robin," Cornysh employs a compositional device familiar in his time: the accompaniment of a melody with a pes, or ground bass. Cornysh's pes is canonic, consisting of two 4-bar phrases with the second voice entering after the fourth measure. The text, "Ah robin, gentle Robin, tell me how thy leman does and thou shalt know of mine," was written by poet Thomas Wyatt (c. 1503–1542). Shakespeare used a modified version of Wyatt's text in *Twelfth Night*, Act IV, scene 2, where Feste mocks the captive Malvolio. Shakespeare often quoted lyrics of songs popular in his day, and it is possible that Cornysh's melody may have been sung in Shakespeare's production of the play, albeit in fragments given the nature of the dialog.

A ground bass, sometimes simply called a ground, is a repeating figure which provides the harmonic structure for a melody. In Cornysh's day, it was not necessarily a low voice, though by the Baroque era this would become the norm.[15] A ground bass did not have to be canonic.

In this setting, the pes or ground can be played by any combination of C recorders. The first group begins, playing for four measures, at which point the second pes group enters. When the first group had played eight measures, the melody (alto) enters. All three parts then play straight through to the end.

The major chord which is heard at the end of every phrase is known as a "picardy" third. It was a common harmonic device in renaissance music. Those playing the alto melody must pay attention to the accidentals, since there are frequent changes between E♮ and E♭, and between B♭ and B♮.

William Cornysh (also spelled Cornish and Cornyshe) was a composer, poet and actor of the English renaissance and a favorite of King Henry VIII of England. Cornysh composed a large number of madrigals and songs, both sacred and secular, as well as motets, masses, and other religious choral music. The oldest known version of "Ah Robin" is from a song book once owned by Henry, known simply as *The Henry VIII Manuscript*.

---

15 A familiar example of a ground bass in the Baroque is the cello part for Johann Pachelbel's "Canon in D," beloved by brides, hated by cellists.

57. Palomita - Mexican folk song
(SAT or SAB)

"Palomita" is a love song; the title means "little dove." In this arrangement the melody is shared by all three voices; none can be omitted. The third voice can be played on tenor or bass.

Students might find the accidentals in the soprano line (measures 20–22) difficult at first. The sound of these raised lower neighbors is common in much Mexican folk music. The tenor part reaches low C in measures 17 and 18, but the rhythms here are slow and there is plenty of time to find finger 7. The bass part crosses the register break in several places and is probably the most difficult of the three parts.

58. O Mitissima/Virgo Virginum/Haec Dies
Bamberg Codex, 13th century
(SSA or SST; SSB)

This motet is an example of medieval parody writing and employs a number of compositional techniques characteristic of the late middle ages.

It is important to note that the word "parody" in this context does not mean "mocking" but rather indicates that new lyrics have been written to be sung to a pre-existent melody. This was a common practice in the middle ages. A better term might be "imitative" or "borrowed" composition. In this piece, the Latin motet was given new secular lyrics in French. In addition, the original motet is polytextual, meaning that the music has more than one set of lyrics, which are sung simultaneously.

Latin lyrics:

Triplum (top line)
O mitissima Virgo Maria Posce tuum filium Ut nobis auxilium Dei et remedium Contra demonum Fallibis les astucias Et horum nequicias.

Motetus (second line):
Virgo virginum, Lumen luminum, Reformatrix hominum, Quae portasti Dominum: Per te, Maria, Detur venia, Angelo nunciante, Virgo es post et ante.

Tenor (bottom two lines):
Haec dies.

Secular French lyrics:
Quant voi revenir D'esté la saison Que le bois font retentir Tuit cil oisillon Adonc pleur et souspir Pour le grant desir Qu'ai de la bele Marion, Qui mon cuer a en prison.

In *Quant voi revenir*, the religious motet appealing to the Virgin Mary for spiritual aid has been transformed into a love song. A young man in springtime (when else?) finds his heart filled with desire for his beloved Marion. Note the word play with the names (Mary/Marion) and the fact that Marion is also the stock name used for a young shepherdess in secular pastoral plays of the middle ages. In other times, such parodying of a sacred song might have been considered sacrilegious, but in medieval thought earthly love was seen as a reflection of divine love, and the shepherdess Marion could easily have been viewed as an analog for the Virgin Mary, mother of the divine shepherd. Devotion to Marion was therefore synonymous with devotion to Mary. Nevertheless, scholars assume that if the secular words were sung (outside the church, of course) the cantus firmus would have been played on instruments rather than sung.

This motet uses a well-known chant as a cantus firmus, or fixed voice. This was a compositional technique in which an existing melody (here the Gregorian chant *Haec Dies*) was sung in the tenor and used as a foundation for other voices. In *O Mitissima/Virgo Virginum*, the cantus firmus is given an isorhythmic treatment, meaning that instead of being sung smoothly and freely as they would be in plainchant style, the notes are given a set and repeating rhythm which provides metric structure for the free-composed lines above it. In the 13th century, plainchant was typically used for a cantus firmus. By the 15th century, the use of popular secular songs became common.

The harmonies in *O Mitissima/Virgo Virginum* exemplify the medieval ideal of open fourths and fifths at beginnings and endings, with relatively little concern about dissonances that may occur between. With regard to harmony, medieval music followed a completely different set of "rules" than music of later periods. If you listen to pieces like this long enough, you will begin to have a different experience of harmony in which the open perfect intervals (fourths, fifths, and octaves) feel uplifting, whereas the thirds (which are a defining characteristic of tonal music from the 16th century through modern times) sound jarring by contrast.

I have included the beginning of *Haec Dies* so that students can see the basis for the tenor, even though it would not have been sung together with the motet.

59. Wenn Ich Ein Vöglein Wär - *Clara Schumann*
(any combination of S, A, and T, with optional B)

Clara Schumann and her husband Robert were so famously devoted to one another that I have to wonder if Clara wrote this little round as a gift to Robert. The lyrics, *Wenn ich ein Vöglein wär, und auch zwei Flügel hätt, flög ich zu dir, zu dir* (If I were a little bird and also had two wings, I would fly to you, to you) seem to make it a musical endearment. Both Clara and Robert were piano virtuosi and creators of large-scale compositions. Even their lieder (songs) have elaborate piano accompaniments. Consequently, I never considered including music of either in this volume until I came across this piece. I have transposed it to F Major so that it can be played on any combination of recorders. With a range of a major tenth, the tune goes into the partial thumb register for C recorders and reaches the lowest note on F recorders.

The lyrics and the beginning of the melody come from an old German or Swiss folk song. The most frequently used version of the text was written by Johann Gottfried Herder (1744–1803) and first published in 1778/79. It has been set to music by many composers.

Clara Schumann, née Wieck, was a piano prodigy who began concertizing at the age of nine. Her performing career spanned more than 60 years, and she had great influence on other pianists both through her teaching and through her programming. She eschewed bombastic virtuosity in favor of sensitive musicianship, and she also reintroduced the works of Baroque masters like Bach and Scarlatti.

In 1840, Clara married pianist and composer Robert Schumann, whom she had met when she was a child and who had also been a student of her father. Clara and Robert were partners not only in marriage, but also in their careers. The couple had eight children together, and both were extremely busy with concert performances. Throughout their life together, Robert was plagued by psychological crises, and in 1854 he experienced a complete breakdown. He attempted suicide and was admitted to a sanatorium where he spent the next two years, ultimately dying of pneumonia in the asylum at the age of 46.

After Robert's hospitalization, Clara became the sole provider for the family, which included her six surviving children, and later two orphaned grandchildren. She supported them by concertizing and teaching. She championed the music of her contemporaries, notably Chopin, Brahms (who was a personal friend), Mendelssohn, and her husband. Her own compositions were rarely performed by anyone other than herself, and after her death remained relatively unheard until the late 20th century. Many of her students went on to have successful careers as performers and teachers, carrying on her legacy of placing musicality and expression over virtuosic display.

Clara Schumann died of a stroke at the age of 72, and at her own request was buried next to Robert.

60. Pinks and Lilies - English country dance tune from The Dancing Master (1726)
(SAT)

"Pinks and Lilies" was a popular dance in 18th-century England. It is danced in a "longways" formation by any number of couples.[16]

Because of its sprightly character, I have arranged this song for treble clef instruments only. The low Cs in the tenor part may be difficult for students to reach, but since they are preceded by Gs and followed by rests they should be manageable. Students who cannot reach finger 7 may take the low Cs in the tenor part up an octave.

A facsimile of the original edition with dance instructions can be seen at https://playforddances.com/dances-2-3/pinks-and-lilies/

61. Mi Y'malel - traditional Hanukkah song
(SAT)

"Mi Y'malel" retells the deeds of the Maccabees in the revolt against Syrian occupation and the rule of King Antiochus IV in 167–160 BCE. Antiochus had ordered that a statue of Zeus be placed in the Jewish temple and had banned a number of important Jewish rites and rituals.

I have given the primary theme an imitative treatment, which allows each of the three voices to play the opening motif. In the final section, the order of entrances is reversed, giving the entire melody to the tenor. The middle section is difficult for soprano because of the augmented seconds between A♭ and B♮. Because the primary melodic material is distributed among the three parts, none can be omitted.

62. Bigi Kaiman - Surinamese folk song
(SAT)

Bigi Kaiman is an example of kaseko, a musical genre that originated in Suriname. Kaseko blends African, European, and American folk idioms into a unique sound. Kaseko songs are rhythmically complex, often involve an element of call-and-response, and are typically accompanied by an assortment of percussion instruments.

---

16 A longwise set consists of two parallel lines of dancers with partners facing each other.

In "Bigi Kaiman" I have used the rhythm of the second section to create a syncopated accompaniment throughout. It is easy to over-blow quick rhythms like these. The notes should be lightly articulated with the tongue, and the air pressure that builds up behind the tongue is enough to make the note sound. Blowing air on every note will be too much, and the instruments will squawk or, at a minimum, the notes will be too sharp and the tone harsh. Students should breathe only when necessary, not during every rest. Breathing too frequently will make them light-headed and slow the tempo.

The lyrics of this song mean "Big Caiman jumps into the water and shouts, 'Beware!'" The caiman is a genus of alligatorid reptile native to Central and South America. There are six different species of caiman.

63. Miserere Nostri Domine - from Pammelia (1609)
Thomas Ravenscroft (c. 1582-c. 1635)
(any combination of S, A and T, with optional B)

Thomas Ravenscroft, perhaps more than any other composer, helped to establish the place of rounds in the English song repertory. He is recognized primarily for his three song collections: *Pammelia* (1609), *Deuteromelia* (1609), and *Melismata* (1611). His early years are largely undocumented. Even the year of his birth is unknown. A chorister named Thomas Ravenscroft is recorded as having sung at St Paul's Cathedral from 1594 to 1600. There is no proof that this is the same person, but it seems highly likely.

Ravenscroft received a bachelor's degree from the University of Cambridge in 1605 and published his first music anthologies four years later. He wrote two treatises on music theory and composed several hymns. He is credited with composing the earliest known song cycle in English music history, a collection of songs called *Hodge and Malkyn* which was published in in 1614 in a book with the rather bewildering title, *The Briefe Discourse of the True (but Neglected) Use of Charact'ring the Degrees*.

Ravenscroft wrote canons and rounds using both secular and sacred texts. All three parts of "Miserere Nostri Domine" can be played on any treble clef recorder, though the altos will need to take the low Ds up an octave, playing the parenthetical notes instead. The third segment of the round moves into the high register for soprano and tenor. The optional bass part doubles the third voice.

64. All Into Service - canon in three parts, from Pammelia
Thomas Ravenscroft (c. 1582-c. 1635)

(any combination of S, A and T, with optional B)

This canon is tricky to play. The entrances do not align with the phrases, and the phrases are of varying lengths. In addition, notes tied across the bar line can be difficult to count, especially since the other two voices change notes on the downbeat.

The text aligns consistently with the melody. The slurred notes in the third to fourth measures of the tune correspond to the word "tole." The spelling below is as it appears in the original publication.

All into \ service, \ the belles to-\le, All into \ service \ now ring they all \ into service; \ Dong dong dong \ bell, ding dong bell. \ (repeat)

For biographical information about Ravenscroft, see #63, "Miserere Nostri Domine."

65. Boomba - Brazilian folk song
(SAT or SAB; SA)

This is not "La Bamba," the Mexican song popularized by Ritchie Valens in 1958, but it is every bit as fun. The syncopations that run throughout melody and accompaniment give it an effervescent character and add challenge to its playing. Fast rhythms must be articulated lightly with the tongue. It is easy to overblow these notes. Generally, there is enough air pressure behind the tongue to make the notes sound without the need to push air from the lungs on every note.

66. Troika - Russian folk dance tune
(SAT; SAB)

A troika is a vigorous dance from Russia in which the dancers' high steps imitate horses pulling a sleigh through deep snow. In this traditional tune, the G♯s bring challenge to all parts. In addition, all parts have wide ranges. However, the music is so engaging that students will be motivated to overcome these challenges. The tenor and bass parts are identical, with the exception of some octave displacements in the bass (eliminating some jumps). The tenor part is more accessible, and the leaps in the tenor voice add energy to the music.

67. A Southerly Wind and Cloudy Sky
anonymous round in three parts
(any combination of S, A, and T)

Light, quick tonguing is the key to playing this lively round well. I have scored it for only treble clef recorders because the long phrases and fast rhythms are not conducive to being played on the bass. Played on alto, the music reaches the lowest note and requires frequent use of finger 7. Played on soprano or tenor it extends into the partial thumb register.

This is a fun round for singing. Since hunting on horseback is not something today's youth are likely to relate to, I think a teacher would be justified in changing the activity to sailing, hiking, or something else relevant to their students. It would then make sense to change "horse" and possibly "Tally ho!" as well.

(1) *A \ southerly wind and a \ cloudy sky pro-\claim it a hunting \ morning; be-\fore the sun rises a-\way we'll fly, dull \ sleep and a downy bed \ scorning.*
(2) *To \ horse, my brave boys, and a-\way! Bright \ Phoebus the hills is a-\dorning; The \ face of all nature looks \ gay; 'tis a \ beautiful hunting \ morning.*
(3) *Then \ hark! Hark! \ forward; Tally \ ho! Tally ho! Tally \ ho! Then \ hark! Hark! \ forward; Tally \ ho! Tally ho! Tally \ ho!*

68. Shake the Papaya Down
traditional Jamaican round in three parts
(any combination of S, A, and T, with optional B)

In this setting the round itself (top line) can be played on any treble clef recorder. It lies most comfortably on alto; on soprano and tenor it extends into the partial thumb register. I have added an optional bass part in the style of a ground bass (see notes for #56, "Ah Robin, Gentle Robin") so that students learning to play bass can be given the opportunity to participate on that instrument.

(1) *Mama says no play, \ this is a work day,\ Up with the bright sun; \ get all the work done. \ If you will help me, \ climb up the tall tree, \ shake the papaya \ down. *
(2) *Shake them down, \ shake them down, \ climb the tall tree,\ shake them down. \ Shake them down, \ shake them down, \ shake the papaya \ down. *
(3) *I love papaya, \ yes I do, \ juicy papaya, \ yes I do. \ If you will help me, \ I'll help you. \ Shake the papaya \ down. *

The first section of the round has new lyrics for a second verse. The second and third sections are the same:
(1) *Sweet, sweet papaya, \ fruit of the island, \ when all the work's done \ dance on the white sands. \ If you will help me, \ climb up the tall tree, \ shake the papaya \ down. *

69. At Summer Morn - anonymous round in three parts
(any combination of S, A, and T, with optional B)

This is an excellent song for waking middle schoolers up in the morning. The seven bar phrases in this round may challenge students who have become accustomed to four and eight bar groups, requiring them to think quickly in order to start the next phrase on time. When played on C recorders, the tune crosses the register break several times. It lies quite comfortably on alto with the exception of one low F♮. I have added a modified bass part that follows the melody's outline but omits the wide leaps in the first segment and is rhythmically easier to play.

The lyrics are below:
(1) *At \ sum–mer \ morn– the \ mer–ry \ lark \ her–alds \ in the \ day.* (2) *At \ even-\tide sad \ Philo-\mel \ breathes– her \ plain–tive \ lay, \ (3) warb- \ling \ sweet-\ly \ all– her \ cares– a-\way.* (repeat)

70. Up and Down This World Goes Round - Matthew Locke (1621-1677)
(any combination of S, A, and T, with optional B)

Matthew Locke was an English composer of the Baroque era who worked in service of King Charles II. His titles included "Composer of the Wind Music – music for the King's sackbutts and cornets"[17] and "Composer for the Violins." He also was organist for the chapel of Queen Catherine. Locke wrote an important treatise on music theory, and he was so highly regarded that Henry Purcell composed an ode on his death entitled "What hope for us remains, now he is gone?"

"Up and Down" is written in the mixolydian mode, a major key with a lowered seventh (in this case F♮ in the key of G). The mixolydian mode is common in folk music from the British Isles.

The lyrics are:
(1) *Up and down this \ world goes round, \ (2) Down, the \ world goes up and \ (3) down, up and \ down the world goes* (repeat)

The round ends with each voice playing the first note of a phrase. The composer seems to have indulged in a bit of word painting in this piece; the melody descends when the word is "down" and it climbs when the word is "up." At the final cadence, one voice has "up" on the highest note in the tune, while the other two have "down" on low notes.

---

17 The sackbutt is an early instrument similar to today's trombone. The cornet was essentially a valveless trumpet.

71. Karaguna - Greek folk dance tune
(SAA, SAT, or STT)

The augmented fourth from E to A♯ and the augmented second from G to A♯ give "Karaguna" an exotic character and could be the result of middle eastern influence. The fingering for A♯ is generally the same as the fingering for B♭, though for this situation I like the sound of the trill fingering (T/1O3/OOOO on C recorders, T/123/4O5O on altos), which is slightly sharper and heightens the harmonic tension. The change from G♮ to G♯ in measure 5 of the soprano part is likely to need extra attention. The middle voice can be played on either alto or tenor; on tenor it extends into the partial thumb register. The three eighth notes at the end of the middle voice serve to link back to the da capo. The fingerings are tricky when played on alto, but easier on tenor. These notes may be omitted if they are too difficult. The third voice can be played on either alto or tenor, but because of the low F♯s, it lies better on tenor.

72. A Voyage to the Moon - Jacques Offenbach (1819-1880)
(SAT)

The son of a synagogue cantor, Jacques Offenbach was born in Prussia (now Germany) and moved to France in 1833 to study at the Paris Conservatory. He began his musical career as a virtuoso cellist, even performing at Windsor Palace for Queen Victoria, Prince Albert, and Emperor Nicholas I of Russia. In the 1850s he began to shift his focus to composing opera, and he would eventually write nearly 100 large-scale works for the stage.

Offenbach met with great success in Paris until the Franco-Prussian War broke out in 1870. Already suspect because of his Jewish heritage, he was now vilified by many for his Prussian birth and accused of being in the service of the Prussian government. Ironically, in Prussia he was scorned and accused of writing songs that denigrated his homeland. Offenbach took his family to safety in Spain until the end of the war, only returning to Paris late in 1871.

Offenbach's music was banned by the Nazis in the 1930s, along with that of Felix Mendelssohn, George Gershwin, and Irving Berlin.

Composed in 1875, *Le voyage dans la lune* (a voyage to the moon) is very loosely based on Jules Verne's 1865 novel *De la Terre à la Lune* (*From the Earth to the Moon*). After the premier, Verne complained about the similarities between his book and the opera, but the issue never rose to the level of legal action. *A Voyage to the Moon* is of a genre known as "opéra-féerie," opera-ballets based on fairy tales or stories involving magic. The story's whimsical nature is immediately evident in the names of its main characters: King Vlan, who rules a fictitious kingdom on Earth; his son Prince Caprice; and the scientist Microscope who invents the cannon that will send the three of them to the moon. Arriving on the moon, they meet King Cosmos; his chief advisor, Cactus; Quipasseria, who controls the lunar "stock market"; and Princess Fantasia. Needless to say, Caprice and Fantasia fall in love, and there are melodramatic scenes galore.

This excerpt from the overture begins with a lyric melody in the tenor accompanied by undulating harmonies in the soprano and alto parts (the melody is played by the French horn in the original orchestration). This is followed by a lively section that presages the comic elements in the plot. The marking *animato* means animated, but the section does not necessarily need to be faster.

The measures in the soprano part that alternate between B and D are most easily played using the trill fingering for B♮ (T/O23/OOOO). This eliminates the awkwardness of moving finger 2 in opposition to finger 1 and the thumb. Chromaticism in the animato section makes the soprano and alto parts challenging.

73. Shosholoza - Zimbabwean folk song
(SAT)

"Shosholoza" is a song from Zimbabwe that was sung by miners working in the gold and diamond mines of South Africa. It is a call-and-response with lyrics in various African languages. Mine workers in South Africa came by train from all around the region. A work song, "Shosholoza" helped keep up the spirits of those engaged in the tedious and dangerous work of mining. Nelson Mandela (1907–2013), who served as president of South Africa from 1994–1999, sang the song as he worked during his imprisonment from 1956 to 1961. To him, the workers' train described in the song was an analog for the anti-apartheid struggle of Black South Africans. Today the song is sometimes referred to as South Africa's second national anthem.

There are many versions of the song. This arrangement blends various renditions by African singers. Although the notes are not difficult, the rhythms are complex and require careful counting and listening. In many places, the parts do not align rhythmically, and students who tend to play by ear may be inclined to follow a different part.

74. Honor to the Hills - *Jeremiah Ingalls (1764-1838)*
(SAT or SAB)

Jeremiah Ingalls was born in Andover, Massachusetts and lived much of his life in Vermont, where he was a church choirmaster.[18] He published *The Christian Harmony* in 1805. "Honor to the Hills" is found in this collection. Although *The Christian Harmony* is not written using shape notes (see notes to #43, "Star in the East"), a derivative hymn from the later publication *Southern Harmony* is, and performing "Honor to the Hills" in shape note style is totally appropriate. Because of the wide range of the middle voice, I arranged "Honor to the Hills" for SAT or SAB. However, one can imitate the sound of shape note singing by doubling the soprano line with alto recorders and the alto line with sopranos, provided there are soprano players able to reach high B♭ (Ø/12O/456O).

"Honor to the Hills" celebrates the presence of God in the natural world. The open fifths and parallel voicing are characteristic of 18th- and early 19th-century American vocal music. Composers like Ingalls rejected the norms of European tonal harmony. Other than having a tonal center, music of this type has little in common with the music of Beethoven or Schubert, who lived at the same time.

75. Marche pour Nérée - *from Cephale et Procris*
Élisabeth Jacquet de la Guerre (1665-1729)
(SAB or STB; SB)

French composer Élisabeth Jacquet de la Guerre lived during the reign of the Louis XIV. She was renowned as a harpsichord virtuoso who could improvise in concert for hours at a time. She composed keyboard suites, chamber music, and operas. *Cephale et Procris* is based on a Greek myth. The "March for Nereus" is heard in the prolog to the opera. A prolog in a 17th-century opera was a bit of a conundrum; it was indispensable, yet it had nothing to do with the story being told. This is because a composer's livelihood was dependent on being in the good graces of the king, and the best way to stay on Louis XIV's good side was flattery. In the prolog, several characters, in this case an assortment of Greek and Roman gods and nymphs, come on stage to dance and sing the praises of his majesty the king, may he live a long life and continue to give us money. Actually, they were a bit more subtle than that, but only a little.

Sadly for Jacquet de la Guerre, and for us as well, the king's interest in opera began to wane, owing in part to the distraction of a war with Spain, and in part the disapproval of his second wife, who was extremely conservative and religious and viewed musical theater as a frivolous waste.

---

18 He also worked as a farmer, barrel maker, and tavern keeper, and was recognized as a skilled player of the bass viola da gamba.

Another barrier to Jacquet de la Guerre's success was sexism. Although she had rich and powerful patrons like the king, many of the better librettists were unwilling to collaborate with a woman. Consequently, the operas for which she wrote some exceptional music suffered from weak text and incoherent plots.

A considerable portion of the soprano line in this setting lies above the register break. The middle voice, when played on tenor, also crosses the break; it is more readily played on alto. Though it also has notes in the partial thumb range, the bass part is relatively straightforward.

Students should already be familiar with dotted rhythms. In this piece there are several doubly dotted half notes (e.g., in measure 2). In this notation, the second dot adds half the value of the first dot.

76. Wee Be Three Poore Mariners - from Deuteromelia
Thomas Ravenscroft (c.1582-c. 1635)
(SAT or SAB)

For biographical information about Thomas Ravenscroft, see #63, "Miserere Nostri Domine." In addition to being a great composer of canons, Ravenscroft wrote a number of madrigal-like songs in parts. "Wee Be Three Poore Mariners" is one. It is found in *Deuteromelia*, published in 1609, where it is listed as a "Freemans song in three parts."

The lyrics are below:
(first verse) *Wee be three poore \ Mariners, new-\ly– come from the \ seas, Wee \ spend our lives in \ jeopardy– whiles \ others live at \ ease, Shall we goe \ daunce the round, the round, the \ round, and shall we goe \ daunce the round, the round, the \ round, and \ he that is a \ bully boy–, come \ pledge me on– the \ ground, the ground, the ground.*

(second verse) *We \ care not for those \ martiall men, that \ doe our states dis-\ daine: But \ we care for those \ Marchant men–, which \ doe our states main-\ taine. To them we \ daunce (etc.)*

Singing the second verse requires a few fairly obvious rhythmic adjustments. The "martiall men" in question would be marines, soldiers for hire that were paid to sail on merchant ships and protect them in the event of a pirate attack. The marines looked down upon the ship's crew and reportedly considered it beneath their dignity to assist in any maritime activities, even in situations where "all hands" were needed to save ship and crew.

77. Feldblumen (H. 169) - Fanny Mendelssohn (1805-1847)
(SAT)

Fanny Mendelssohn was an accomplished pianist and composer whose music was largely unpublished during her lifetime. Despite encouraging Fanny to study music, her parents, in accord with the social conventions of the time, discouraged public performance or the publication of her music. Fanny was, however, very close to her younger brother Felix, and in 1826 and 1827 the pair conspired to include six of Fanny's songs in Felix's Op. 8 and Op. 9. The deception would not have been difficult; their compositional styles were very similar, as might be expected with siblings having the same piano and composition teachers. It was a bit of a problem, however, when Queen Victoria of England hosted Felix at Buckingham Palace and announced that she intended to sing her favorite of his *lieder* (songs); it was one that Fanny had written, and Felix admitted their subterfuge.

Throughout his life, Felix expressed that he believed Fanny to be the better pianist, and he never submitted a work for publication unless Fanny had approved it first. Letters between the two confirm that Felix consistently incorporated Fanny's recommendations into his final versions.

There is a measure of inconsistency among publishers as to how they refer to both Fanny and Felix. The family was Jewish, and their father, Abraham, believed that Jews should assimilate into German society, partly because he realized that adherence to Jewish faith and traditions greatly limited one's opportunities. His brother-in-law, Jakob Salomon Bartholdy, had taken the surname Bartholdy from a property he had acquired, in hopes of masking his Jewish roots. He persuaded Abraham to do the same. In 1816, Fanny and her siblings were baptized as Protestant Christians.[19] Fanny was baptized Fanny Cäcilie Mendelssohn Bartholdy. Both Fanny and Felix objected to the name change, expressing a strong dislike for "Bartholdy." Nevertheless, when Fanny published her Op. 1 songs in 1846, it was under the name "Fanny Hensel geb. Mendelssohn-Bartholdy."[20] Another reason Abraham chose to adopt a new family name was the fact that his father, Moses Mendelssohn, was a renowned philosopher. Abraham once remarked that he had the misfortune of being the son of a famous father and the father of a famous son.

The Mendelssohn family had a history of stroke, and on May 14, 1847 Fanny, at the age of 42, experienced a fatal stroke during a rehearsal of one of Felix's cantatas. Felix was devastated by the loss of his sister. He set about gathering

---

[19] Abraham and his wife Lea were not baptized until 1822.

[20] geb. is an abbreviation of *geboren*, the German equivalent of "née." Fanny's husband was the artist Wilhelm Hensel. Hensel not only approved of Fanny composing and publishing her music, but also encouraged it.

her compositions and submitting them to his publisher, Breitkopf & Härtel, for publication, but, before he could complete this process, Felix also suffered a series of strokes and died at the age of 38, six months after the death of his sister. In 1850, Breitkopf & Härtel began publishing Fanny's music. Her total output included 250 lieder (songs), 125 works for piano, four cantatas, an orchestral overture, and several chamber works.

"Feldblumen" (field flowers) is one of a posthumously published collection of choral songs entitled *Feldlied*. Since it was written in 1826, before Fanny's marriage, I have identified her as "Fanny Mendelssohn" rather than "Fanny Hensel." The song is for SATB chorus, but I have excerpted a section written for three solo voices and transposed it from E Major to C Major to make the music accessible to recorders. The alto part is quite chromatic and challenging. The tenor part also has some tricky spots involving simultaneous finger changes.

78. Sonata Prima - *first movement*
Isabella Leonarda (1620-1704)

(SSB)

Born in Novara to a prominent and influential family, Isabella Leonarda became a nun at age 16 and was later recognized as a composer of great talent. Her first publication was in 1640, when she was but 20 years old, and she continued composing and publishing for the next sixty years, making her one of the most prolific female composers of the Baroque era. Most of her music was written when she was over the age of 50.

Leonarda wrote mostly religious music, the solo motet being her preferred genre. She was the first woman to publish instrumental sonatas, these being published in 1693 as Op. 16. She had formal education in counterpoint, and her skill in this area is evident in the sonata movement presented here. Some of her sonatas follow the standard four-movement format, but others are much more experimental in form. Even those with four movements do not follow the typical slow-fast-slow-fast structure. The movement structure of "Sonata Prima" is Allegro/Largo/Adagio/Aria Allegro/Vivace. It was originally written for two violins and violone,[21] but like many instrumental works of the Baroque it is readily playable on other instruments, including recorders. In this sonata, the three instruments are equal partners, each playing both principal and supporting roles.

---

21 The violone is an early bowed string instrument in the bass register. In the Baroque era, the term was often applied to the double bass viol, but might also have designated other bowed bass instruments. Leonarda's instrumentation also called for "organo" or organ. No separate part was written for the organ. Rather, the organist, or any keyboard player for that matter, would read the bass part and improvise the right hand to fill in harmonies, rather like jazz musicians today. Like most sonatas of the period, Leonarda's Op. 16 sonatas sound complete with or without keyboard.

79. Were You There? - *African-American spiritual*
(SAT; SA)

I have given this spiritual a jazzy/bluesy harmonization. Blues and jazz are uniquely American genres that developed out of African-American musical traditions. When sung as a hymn, "Were You There?" often is treated as a call-and-response, with the response "Were you there?" coming during the long note at the end of every phrase. I have imitated this by inserting a chromatic motif in the alto (and sometimes also in the tenor) at these moments. The idea is for it to sound like a gospel singer seizing a moment of inspiration to improvise a response to the preceding phrase.

Since most of the thirds and blues notes are in the alto part, "Were You There?" can be successfully performed with just sopranos and altos. If this is done, the alto players should divide between the alto and tenor notes in the final two measures. If the piece is played with just one soprano and one alto, the tenor notes are preferred at the end. The level of chromaticism in all parts make this arrangement pretty challenging, but older students will enjoy and be motivated by the style.

80. The Echo - *anonymous round in three parts*
(any combination of S, A, and T, with optional B)

In the key of C Major, as it is written here, this whimsical round lies quite comfortably on F recorders, but less so on C recorders. On soprano and tenor, the first and third segments of the round are largely in the partial thumb register. The bass doubles the third voice an octave lower. "The Echo" may be played with any combination of treble clef recorders as well as with the optional bass.

The entrances are tricky because the first segment of the round is not completed until after the second voice's entrance. Students must count rests carefully.

When all voices are playing, an echo-like effect (C-B; G-E) can be heard beginning in measure 6. The lyrics are below:
In– \ for–est– green the \ e-cho– sounds and– \ ev'rything re-\sounds, come \ here, oh \ come you all \ come here, \ oh, come, \ you all! (repeat)

PART C - Music in Four Parts

Most of the music in this section is written or arranged for the standard SATB combination. Some can be performed with reduced instrumentation, but most require all four parts. The last several pieces in this section are quite difficult, involving wide ranges, extensive chromaticism, difficult fingerings, and complex rhythms.

81. Kommt und Laßt Uns Tanzen
anonymous round in four parts
(any combination of S, A, T, and B)

This round is easy to play on any recorder. It is useful for students learning to play tenor and bass. The German lyrics, *Kommt und \ laßt uns \ tanzen, \ springen, \ kommt und \ laßt uns \ frölich sein* align exactly with the notes of the melody. The use of "kommt" and "laßt" is not consistent with modern German, which would use "komm" and "lass." A singable English translation is: *Come and \ let us \ dance and \ spring–,\ come and \ let us \ mer-ry \ be.*

82. Glaube und Hoffe! (WoO 174)
Ludwig van Beethoven (1779-1827)
(SATB)

Although Breitkopf and Härtel published this little piece in a set of 5 canons, it is not really a canon; just canon-like. The piece was written as a gift to Moritz Adolf Schlesinger, son of a Berlin music publisher. According to Schlesinger, he had been invited to meet Beethoven, but found the composer in a terrible temper. Beethoven had supposedly ordered roast veal for dinner and had been told none was available. Schlesinger hurried home, procured some roast veal, and had it delivered to Beethoven. "Glaube und Hoffe!" was, according to Schlesinger, written as a "thank-you." Whether or not the story is precisely true (Schlesinger told it to Beethoven's biographer some 40 years later, so it's possible that the tale might have been embellished in his memory), it is easy to imagine Beethoven reacting to the situation in this way. He was famously mercurial in mood, and often disposed to anger.

The WoO designation stands for "without opus" and is used for music not published by the composer. "Glaube und hoffe" translates to "believe and hope."

The fingering transitions to E♭ in the soprano and tenor parts are a bit tricky, and the low F and low B♭ in the alto and bass parts respectively require the use of finger 7. Otherwise the piece is quite manageable and short enough to be easily learned.

83. Da Pacem Domine - Melchior Franck (c. 1580-1639)
canon in four parts at the lower fifth
(SATB)

This motet is an example of a canon at the lower fifth; the second and fourth voices sing or play exactly the same melody as the first and third, only beginning on the fifth scale degree (in this case, on D rather than G). The melody's narrow range helps make it easy to play.

A prolific composer, Franck wrote over 600 motets. He was also quite versatile, writing music in a variety of styles. In music history, he stands as a prominent figure bridging between the Renaissance and Baroque eras.

84. Samba Lele - Brazilian children's song
(SATB; SAT; SAA; SA; or ST)

The short staccato rhythms in the accompanying voices are easily overblown. The build-up of air behind the tongue should be enough to produce the tone. Blowing on every note is too much. It is also not necessary to breathe during every rest. Breathing too often can lead to light-headedness.

The third voice, marked A/T, can be played on either alto or tenor, though tenor is easier. If only soprano and alto instruments are available, the SAA version is preferable to the SA. If the piece is played with just two parts, the first and third lines should be used.

85. Down, Down, Down - Pennsylvania coal mining ballad
(SATB or SAT)

"Down, Down, Down" was passed by word of mouth from miner to miner until the 1920s, when it was written down by George Korson and published in his book, *Songs and Ballads of the Anthracite Miners*. I have included lyrics for the first two verses here. The rest may be found online at http://www.protestsonglyrics.net/Labor_Union_Songs/Down-Down-Down.phtml.

With your kind attention a song I will trill
All ye who must toil with the pick and the drill,
And sweat for your bread in that hole in Oak Hill,
That goes down, down, down.

When I was a boy said my daddy to me:
"Stay out of the mines, take my warning," said he,
"Or with dust you'll be choked and a pauper you'll be,"
Broken down, down, down.

Among the hardships faced by miners was the company store, which is mentioned later in the song. In many industries, laborers were either required to shop at the company store or were unable to shop elsewhere. This often meant exorbitant prices which drove the laborers into debt to the company, leading to virtual slavery as they strove to work off the debt.

Like "Red Iron Ore" (35), this tune is very similar to "Sweet Betsy from Pike," a song about the California Gold Rush first published in 1858, which was itself derived from an earlier English song called "Villikins and His Dinah," first published in London in 1853 and quite popular in the U.S. "Villikins," in turn, was a parody of "William and Dinah," a popular English broadside ballad dating to circa 1819. This kind of musical borrowing is very common in folk music traditions.

86. Ha Ba Tshameka - Botswanan folk song
(SSSA or SSST)

This song from the southern African nation of Botswana demonstrates two features common to music of this region: call and response, and parallel voice movement. I have arranged it with the alto/tenor giving the calls and the responses being played by three soprano voices.

This piece employs a few difficult rhythm patterns, with some notes sounding before the beat and others tying across bar lines. The notes themselves are not difficult.

Much of Botswana is desert, the Kalahari covering about 70% of its area. The name means "land of the Tswana." The Tswana are a Bantu-speaking ethnic group that migrated to the area around 600 BCE and comprises about 79% of the nation's population. The indigenous inhabitants are believed to be the San, Khoi, and other groups speaking click-languages. When Europeans began colonizing southern Africa, indigenous populations were decimated by disease and genocide. In the 1880s Britain annexed the region that today is Botswana. It was not until 1964 that Botswana regained political independence.

87. As I Mee Walked - canon in four parts
Thomas Ravenscroft (c. 1582-c. 1635)
(SATT or SATB)

As I mee \ walk-ed, \ in a Ma\y[22] morning, \ I heard a \ birde sing\ (rest) \ Cuckow. Ravenscroft used no measure lines, and songs were phrased according to the text. Because of this, when played or sung the music may sound as though the meter is changing.

---
22 The word "May" ties across the bar line.

Ravenscroft's actual voicing of the melody is that which appears in the soprano and tenor lines. In the alto and bass lines, the low C is written up an octave in order to keep the entire piece in the range of F recorders. Students playing the tenor line/s may also play the low C an octave higher if this is more comfortable. Played on C recorders, the high F and high G move into the partial-thumb register. I have added a final "cuckoo" in the upper three lines so that all parts may end together. Those playing the upper voices must count the rests rather than playing by ear.

For biographical information about Ravenscroft, see #63, "Miserere Nostri Domine."

88. Ein Feste Burg Ist Unser Gott - melody by Martin Luther (1483-1546); harmonized by J.S. Bach (1685-1750)
(SATB)

The well-known hymn "Ein Feste Burg Ist Unser Gott" was written by Martin Luther around 1529. Luther argued that liturgical music should be singable by the average church-goer. This sentiment led to his famous (and certainly apocryphal) quip, "Why should the devil get all the good tunes?" The original melody was written in changing meter, but the form most familiar today is the "isorhythmic" version found in many hymnals. That is the form used here. The tune was a favorite among later composers. J.S. Bach used the chorale multiple times in cantatas, oratorios, and organ works. "Ein Feste Burg" has often been referred to as "the battle hymn of the Reformation" because of its effectiveness in drawing supporters to the movement.

The tenor and bass parts in this setting move into the partial-thumb register. The almost continuous eighth notes that shift from one voice to another require careful attention to rhythm. Students who habitually play by ear will be challenged to stay in the right place.

89. Schaut Hin! Dort Liegt im Finstern Stall - from the Christmas Oratorio, BWV 248 - melody by Martin Luther (1483-1546) (Vom Himmel Hoch, c. 1539); harmonized by J.S. Bach (1685-1750)
(SATB)

The lyrics for "Vom Himmel Hoch" were probably written by Martin Luther in 1534. They were first published in the *Klugsches Gesangbuch* in 1535 with the heading "Ein Kinderlied auff die Weinacht Christi, Martinus Luther" (a children's song on the nativity of Christ, Martin Luther). In this publication the text was paired with the tune of a familiar children's song, "Ich komm aus fremden Landen her." This is the only known instance of Luther using a secular song to accompany religious text. The better-known tune, which is presented here, was most likely written by Luther and was published in 1539.

J.S. Bach used "Vom Himmel Hoch" four times in his *Christmas Oratorio*, BWV 248. He also used the melody in the Christmas version of his *Magnificat*, BWV 243a; in four chorale preludes for organ in his *Orgelbüchlein*, BWV 606; and as the theme for his *Canonic Variations on Vom Himmel hoch da komm' ich her*, BWV 769.

As in his setting of "Ein Feste Burg," Bach keeps an almost continuous eighth-note pattern running throughout "Schaut Hin!" This makes it necessary for all players to be attentive to the rhythm of their own part and not simply follow the melody by ear. The bass part is particularly tricky, having a wide range and rhythms that often move independently of the other voices.

90. *El Corrido de Gregorio Cortez* - Mexican folk ballad
(SATB)

From 1821 to 1836 Texas was part of Mexico. In 1836 Texas declared its independence, forming the Republic of Texas. Then, in 1845, Texas was officially annexed by the United States. The Tejanos, Texans of Mexican/Hispanic descent, were now officially citizens of the U.S., but they were treated as second-class citizens. Many worked as tenant farmers, renting the land on which they eked out a living. As "Angelos" moved into Texas from other areas, many assumed that it was acceptable to claim for themselves land that had once belonged to Tejanos and indigenous people. Some even considered it a good thing to kill Mexican-Americans.[23] It was in this environment that Gregorio Cortez lived and became a legend.

Cortez was a tenant farmer who grew corn. In 1901, Cortez was accused of horse theft. He had traded a mare for a male horse, but when asked by sheriff W.T. Morris if he had traded a horse, he answered no, because he had not traded a horse (*caballo*), but rather a mare (*yegua*). The sheriff, believing that Cortez was lying, drew his gun to arrest him for horse theft. Cortez's brother, Romaldo, tried to intervene and was shot by the sheriff. At this point, Gregario Cortez drew his own pistol and fatally shot Morris.

After taking his brother to safety, Cortez took flight and evaded the Texas Rangers for thirteen days. During that time he was pursued by up to 300 men, traveled over 500 miles on horseback and foot, and allegedly killed two more men. He was captured eventually and brought to trial. There would be multiple trials and appeals.

---

23 Alonzo, A.C. (1998), Tejano Legacy: Rancheros and Settlers in South Texas, 1734-1900, Albuquerque: University of New Mexico Press.

The trials were dubious. There were changes in testimony, political and social pressure applied to jurors, and other problems. In one trial Cortez was found guilty of second-degree murder and sentenced to 50 years in prison. In the other he was found guilty of first-degree murder and given a death sentence. Eventually, the first degree conviction was overturned, and Cortez began serving a life sentence in 1905.

During the course of the trials, public outrage was rampant. On one side were those who believed Cortez was guilty and should be executed. On the other were those who believed he had acted in self-defense. Even before the trials began, Mexican-Americans in Texas set up a defense fund through which he was able to hire attorneys. After his conviction, there were public efforts to get him pardoned. A pardon was granted in 1913.

"El Corrido de Gregorio Cortez" tells his story. A corrido is a Mexican ballad, often focused on historical events or on themes of social injustice or hardship. Corridos typically have an instrumental introduction, which may also serve as an interlude between verses. The typical structure of a corrido is eight stanzas, each consisting of four to six lines of eight syllables. I have sought to preserve the basic structure of a corrido in this arrangement, albeit without eight stanzas.

91. Lass Dein' Engel mit Mir Fahren - from Cantata 19, Es Erhub Sich Ein Streit - melody by Louis Bourgeois (1510-1559) (Freu dich sehr, o meine Seele); harmonized by J.S. Bach (1685-1750)
(SATB)

French composer Louis Bourgeois was a primary contributor to the *Genevan Psalter*, also called the *Huguenot Psalter*, of 1539. The hymns in this psalter were largely written with just the melody. John Calvin, who promoted and supervised the production of the psalter, believed (like Martin Luther) that church music should be simple enough to be sung by the congregation.[24] In what may have been an overactive response to the elaborate polyphony of Catholic church music, he also opposed singing hymns in parts. Bourgeois did write harmonies for many of his hymns, but these are simple homophonic settings and seem to have been for use outside the church. Bourgeois is also the composer of the hymn commonly known as "Old 100th" (114, "Vous Saints Ministres du Signeur").

Johann Sebastian Bach wrote Cantata 19, *Es Erhub Sich Ein Streit* (There Arose a War) for performance on the Feast of St Michael on September 29, 1726. It is a dramatic work, beginning with a musical depiction of the battle between the

---

24 Calvin became familiar with the musical ideas of Luther when he moved from Geneva to Strasbourg in 1538.

archangel Michael and Satan, and ending with this chorale reflecting heavenly repose:

> Let your angel travel with me on Elias' red chariot and preserve my soul, like Lazarus after his death. Let my soul rest in your bosom; fill it with joy and consolation until my body comes from the earth and is united with it.[25]

The 3/4 meter of "Lass Dein' Engel" gives it a lilting, soothing quality. This chorale is unusual in that it has a mix of four- and five-bar phrases.

In 1726 Bach had been the director of church music for the city of Leipzig for three years. His responsibilities in Leipzig included providing music for four parishes. The Leipzig years (1723–1750) were some of Bach's most productive, in large part because the churches required a cantata for every Sunday of the year. More than 200 cantatas by Bach exist today. Most of these were composed during the Leipzig period, and there are dozens that he is believed to have written but have been lost.

92. Finlandia Hymn - Jean Sibelius (1864-1957)
(SATB; SAT; SA)

Finlandia is a nationalist tone poem for symphony orchestra composed by Jan Sibelius in 1899–1900. The "Finlandia Hymn" is not (as is sometimes claimed) a Finnish folk melody, but was entirely composed by Sibelius. In the early 20th century, toward the end of the Russian Empire's domination of Finland, *Finlandia* was often performed as an act of protest, albeit under alternative, innocuous sounding titles, due to intensive Russian censorship.

In 1938, Sibelius arranged the hymn theme of *Finlandia* for male chorus as the final movement of his *Masonic Ritual Music*, Op. 113. With various other lyrics, the theme is also used as a hymn in many Christian churches.

The biggest challenge in performing the Finlandia hymn on recorders is breath control. The phrases are long and must be played smoothly.

---

25 Bach Cantatas Website, https://www.bach-cantatas.com/index.htm

93. Go Down, Moses - African-American spiritual
(SATB; SAT)

"Go Down, Moses" was published in 1862 with the title "Oh! Let My People Go," making it the first African-American spiritual put in print.

For this arrangement, I have used the pulsating rhythm of "go down, Moses" to accompany the opening melody in the soprano line. In the refrain, the melody moves first to the alto, then to the tenor, while the soprano plays an imitative descant. The bass part adds depth and harmonic variety to the arrangement, but can be omitted if bass instruments are not available. It could also be played on a cello to good effect.

94. Nous Étions Trois Soldats - French-Canadian voyageur song
(any combination of S, A, and T, with optional B)

Call-and-response songs like this are familiar fare to many whose physical labors must be synchronized with those of others. The call, in the top line, can be played by any treble clef recorder, as can the two middle voices. I have given the bass part simpler rhythms because of the instrument's slower response time.

As is often the case with work songs, there are various versions of lyrics and tune. Here is one version of the lyrics:

(call) *Nous étions \ trois sol-\dats du régi-\ment d'An-\gers*
(response) *Nous étions \ trois sol-\dats du régi-\ment d'An-\gers*
(call) *Pour \ l'amour d'une \ fille, nous \ avons déser-\té–; mon falu-\ron don-\ daine–, mon falu-\ron don-\dé*
(response) *mon falu-\ron don-\daine–, mon falu-\ron don-\dé.*

95. Viva il Nostra Alcide - George Frideric Handel (1685-1759)
from Giulio Cesare in Egitto
(SATB)

Handel wrote the opera *Julius Caesar in Egypt* in 1724. It was given its premier in London that year, and it was such a success that the theater was filled night after night. The plot is loosely based on Caesar's pursuit of Pompey in Egypt. Handel's librettist took great liberties with historical facts, purely for dramatic purposes.

The chorus "Viva il Nostra Alcide" opens the opera. Caesar has defeated Pompey's army, and the Egyptians are awaiting his arrival on the banks of the Nile. The song compares him to Hercules, Alcide being the Greek hero's birth name.

Despite being composed in England for an English audience, the opera was written in Italian, as was the convention of the time. Audiences mostly came to the opera to hear the music, and the plots were simple enough that an understanding of Italian was hardly necessary to follow them.

The dotted rhythms in the soprano part involve some tricky fingering changes, especially in measures 10 and 11, but otherwise the music is not overly difficult. The melody moves to the alto in measure 13 because it goes too low for soprano. This arrangement is drawn from the beginning and end of the chorus, cutting the modulatory middle section.

96. Es Ist Ein' Ros' Entsprungen
Michael Praetorius (1571-1621)
(SATB)

"Lo, how a rose e'er blooming" is arguably Praetorius' best known and most beloved composition, though he is not responsible for the melody. This was first published in the 1599 *Speyer Hymnal*. Other versions of the hymn tune predate the Speyer copy, perhaps going back as far as the time of Martin Luther. The text dates to the 15th century. Praetorius published his harmonization in 1609.

Breath control is very important in playing this piece, as the phrases are long and the melody is lyric. Ideally, breaths should be taken only at the repeat and during rests.

In addition to being a prominent and influential composer, Michael Praetorius wrote three volumes of a treatise on music, *Syntagma Musicum*, which is one of our best sources of information on the music of the early 17th century. His birth name, Michael Schultze, was Latinized to Praetorius, both meaning "magistrate." A devout Lutheran, he wrote his liturgical compositions in German rather than Latin, contributing greatly to the Protestant ideal of making religious music accessible to congregations.

97. Nun Danket Alle Gott - Johann Crüger (1598-1662)
(SATB)

Johann Crüger's importance in music history was largely as the editor of *Praxis Pietatis Melica*, an important Lutheran hymnal of the 17th century. He studied both music and theology, and he composed several hymn tunes, of which "Nun Danket Alle Gott" (now thank we all our God) is perhaps the best known. The melody is simple, yet elegant, and moving quarter notes in the harmony lines provide rhythmic and harmonic variety. The bass part in this setting is perhaps the most difficult, while the soprano is by far the easiest.

98. This Train - *African-American spiritual*
(SATB)

From its roots as an African-American spiritual, "This Train" became a gospel hit in the 1930s. Since then it has been performed and recorded by musicians in virtually every popular music genre. In recognition of the song's gospel and blues history, I have incorporated a number of blues notes and altered chords.

The A♯s in the alto part and the E♯ in the tenor might be unfamiliar. They are generally played with the same fingerings as B♭ and F♮ respectively, though I like the trill fingering (T/123/4O5O for both) as it is slightly sharper and increases the harmonic tension of the altered chord. The F♮ in measure 5 of the tenor part should be played with the standard fingering (T/123/4O67).

99. Dem Bones - *J. Rosamond Johnson (1873-1954)*
(SATB; SAT; SAA; STB; or ST)

This spiritual was included in Volume 1 of this series, but I have also placed it here because of its usefulness to the study of the skeletal system. If the students learned the tune in third grade, they will still enjoy the dissonant jazz chords and blues notes that have been added.

John Rosamond Johnson was a Black American composer and singer of Haitian descent who collaborated with his older brother, poet James Weldon Johnson, in writing songs. Together they wrote "Lift Every Voice and Sing" (136), which came to be known as the Black National Anthem.

Johnson studied music at the New England Conservatory in Boston, and later in London. Together with his brother and Black composer Bob Cole (1868–1911), he created and produced Broadway musicals geared toward both Black and white audiences. Their musicals *Shoo-Fly Regiment* and *Red Moon* had all-Black casts.

Johnson also worked as an editor and arranger. Together with his brother, he compiled and edited four collections of African-American songs: *The Book of American Negro Spirituals, The Second Book of Negro Spirituals, Shoutsongs,*[26] and *Rolling Along in Song.*

As in "This Train" (98), I have used jazz chords to harmonize "Dem Bones," also adding to the end a four-bar sequence of seventh and added-note chords above a G pedal in the bass. If the piece is performed without bass recorder,

---

26 "Shout" is a style of gospel music that is fast, upbeat, and active. It developed in African-American churches, where it was often accompanied by hand clapping and ecstatic dancing.

I recommend having some tenor and/or alto players play their low G in the final four bars. It will be an octave higher than the G in the bass part, but will still be lower than the final notes in the alto and tenor parts.

100. Hot Time in the Old Town (Mrs. O'Leary's Cow)
- Theodore A. Metz (1848-1936)
(SATB; STB; SAT; ST)

Anyone who ever sang this song around a campfire might have trouble believing that it is based on an actual historic tragedy: the Great Chicago Fire of 1871. It also underscores the discrimination against Irish immigrants in the late 19th century.

On the evening of October 8, 1871, a fire broke out in or near the barn of the O'Leary family. An unusually dry summer combined with high winds made conditions perfect for a conflagration. All-wood construction, tar roofs, and wooden sidewalks provided ample fuel. In addition, the predominant building technique of the time, known as "balloon framing," resulted in buildings that acted as one huge chimney flue, allowing flames to race through them. Finally, the city of Chicago, with a population of over 330,000 people, had only 185 firefighters and 17 horse-drawn steam pumpers. Making matters worse, poor communications resulted in the firefighters initially being sent to the wrong location.

The fire burned violently until the evening of October 9, when its fuel began to run out, and when rainfall helped quench the flames. It was days, however, before the city's ruins cooled enough for anyone to assess the damage or search for victims. About 300 people perished in the fire, which also destroyed more than three square miles and over 17,000 buildings. 90,000 people, more than a quarter of the city's residents, were left homeless.

The story of Mrs O'Leary's cow began as one of several rumors about the cause of the fire. Soon after the incident, Michael Ahern, a reporter for the *Chicago Republican*, reported that Mrs O'Leary had been milking the cow and knocked over a lantern. The rumors expanded to include the notion that she was drunk at the time, though Mrs O'Leary testified that she was in bed when the fire started. Daniel Sullivan, the man who reported the fire, said that after he freed the animals from the barn he had gone to the O'Leary house to wake them, thus seeming to confirm Mrs O'Leary's story. Other rumors held that it was Sullivan who started the fire, or that a group of men gambling in the barn had knocked over a lantern. The official report was that the cause of the fire could not be determined.

That, however, was not enough to stop the rumors, and in the court of public opinion Mrs O'Leary and her cow were blamed for the disaster. A popular song called "Hot Time in the Old Town," published by songwriting team Theodore A. Metz and Joe Hayden, was fitted with new lyrics that are now better known than the original.[27] The parody song helped establish the rumor as fact in the popular imagination, and the belief in Mrs O'Leary's guilt continued, despite Michael Ahern's admission in 1893 that he had made up the story.

Mrs O'Leary's tale is one that has been repeated many times with many different groups. Anti-Irish and anti-Catholic sentiments were strong in the mid- to late-19th century. Earlier immigrants, especially those from England, regarded them as lazy, ignorant drunkards. Throughout much of the 19th century, job listings in American newspapers often included the words "no Irish need apply." Since the O'Learys were Irish, it was an easy step for non-Irish people to find them responsible for the fire. The belief in the veracity of the story was pervasive and long lasting. Finally, in 1997, more than a century after Mrs O'Leary's death, the Chicago City Council was persuaded to exonerate her of any guilt.

As with many songs passed by word of mouth, there are various versions. Here are the words as I remember them:

Late one night, when– \ we were all in bed, \ Mrs O'Leary left a \ lantern in the shed, And when the \ cow kicked it over, she \ winked her eye and said, "It'll be a \ hot time in the old town to-\night."

With the exception of the final high G in the soprano, all four parts remain in the low to middle register. The high G is not hard to find, given that it is an octave above the preceding note. The thumb simply needs to shift from closed position to partial-hole. The bigger challenge is getting the appropriate air pressure for the high note. The A♯s in the soprano and tenor parts can be played with the standard B♭ fingering (T/1O3/4OOO), but I prefer the trill fingering (T/1O3/OOOO), both because of the quick rhythm and also because it accentuates the melodic inflection of the note. Use the standard fingering for the B♭ in the first ending; the trill fingering will clash excessively with the C♮ in the alto.

---

27 I say "published by" rather than "written by" because there is some indication that Metz may have heard the song, or a similar song, sung in 1893 by a popular performer known as Mama Lou and copyrighted it in his own name. There are other stories of the song's origin as well.

101. Levellers and Diggers - English folk song
(SATB)

The Levellers and the Diggers were two related socio-political groups of 17th-century England. They rose out of dissatisfaction with economic and political inequities in English society at the time.

The Levellers were organized in 1646, near the end of the English Civil War. The name "Levellers" came from the New Model Army of the roundheads. John Lilburn, an early leader of the movement, objected to its use, preferring instead the term "agitators." The Levellers were initially associated with the roundheads, or Puritans, but later broke from and opposed this faction when it came to power, viewing it as being just as corrupt as the old regime. The Levellers' objectives included religious tolerance; extending voting rights (though not to women, servants, or the poor); abolishing the imprisonment of debtors; and eliminating government corruption. The movement gained a significant following in London, but by 1649 its influence had waned and the organization was dissolved.

The Diggers were an offshoot of the Levellers with more radical ideas that included common ownership of all land. They initially called themselves the "True Levellers," but became known as the Diggers when various groups attempted to grow crops on public lands, declaring this to be their natural right. Their leader, Gerard Winstanley, based his ideology on verses from the Book of Acts describing the conversion of doubters on Pentecost: *And all that believed were together, and had all things common; And sold their possessions and goods, and parted them to all men, as every man had need.*[28] The Diggers' efforts were not well received. There were outbreaks of violence, Digger leaders were arrested, and the Digger movement fell apart after two years.

Despite their common origins and shared disdain for the established order, the Levellers and the Diggers had quite different approaches to equalization. The Levellers, with their emphasis on religious tolerance and voting rights, can be seen as an early attempt at democratization, whereas the Diggers, with their belief in collectivism, were more akin to modern-day Communism.

The lyrics for the song "Levellers and Diggers," also known as "The Diggers' Song," were written by Gerard Winstanley and sung to an existing tune. The melody is a variant of a song genre that includes "Ye Jacobites by Name," "Sam Hall," and "Captain Kidd," all ballads about individuals or groups that defied the established social or political order. The first verses of the song pretty well sum up the Diggers' ideology:

---
28 Acts II, verses 44–45, King James version

*You \ noble Diggers \ all, stand up \ now, stand up \ now, You \ noble Diggers \ all, stand up \ now, \\ Your \ waste lands to main-\tain, seeing \ Cavaliers by \ name Your \ digging to dis-\dain, and your \ persons all de-\fame; Stand up \ now, Diggers \ all. *

*Your \ houses they pull \ down, stand up \ now, stand up \ now, Your \ houses they pull \ down, stand up \ now.\\ Your \ houses they pull \ down to \ fright all men in \ town, But the \ gentry must come \ down, and the \ poor shall wear the \ crown; Stand up \ now, Diggers \ all. *

With \ spades and hoes and \ plows, stand up \ now, stand up \ now, With \ spades and hoes and \ plows, stand up \ now.\\ Your \ freedom to up-\hold, seeing \ Cavaliers are \ bold, To \ kill you if they \ could, and \ rights from you with-\hold; Stand up \ now, Diggers \ all.

The reverse dotted rhythm that is prominent in this song (and eighth note followed by a dotted quarter note) is known as a Scotch snap. It is characteristic of the Scottish country dance called a strathspey and lends rhythmic dynamism to a tune.

With the exception of a single high G in the soprano part, this arrangement stays in the low to middle register for all instruments.

102. By'm Bye - African-American spiritual
(SATB)

This song was first published in Carl Sandburg's *The American Songbag* in 1927. The editor precedes it with these words: "The stealth and mystery of the coming out of the stars one by one on the night sky ... a fragment of a spiritual heard in Texas in the early 1880s by Charley Thorpe of Santa Fe."[29]

The fingerings for the F♮–E♭–E♮–F♮–E♮ sequence at the end of the tenor part are tricky, as are those for the B♮–A♭–G sequence near the end of the alto part. The dropping octaves in the second half of the soprano require that the fingers be set precisely together.

---

29 Sandburg, Carl, *The American Songbag*, Harcourt, Brace and Company, New York, 1927

103. Follow the Drinking Gourd - African-American spiritual
(SATB; SAB; or SAT)

The question of whether this song was used as coded instructions for following the Underground Railroad is debated by scholars. It was first published in 1928 by the Texas Folklore Society. There are no references to the song prior to 1910, when it was collected by folklorist H.B. Parks. Arguments against the song's authenticity include the lack of early versions, the fact that many escapees actually fled to southern cities rather than heading straight north, and also the idea that if the song included verbal instructions (a "verbal map") as claimed, it would not have remained secret for long. It has also been subjected to significant rewriting over the years. Historicity aside, it is still a good song that reflects the longing of enslaved people for freedom.

The drinking gourd referenced in the song is the constellation Ursa Major, or the big dipper, the shape of which resembled a hollowed out gourd such as might have been used for dipping and drinking water. Since two stars in Ursa Major point toward Polaris, the north star, the constellation has long been used in navigation for determining true north. "Follow the Drinking Gourd" became popular during the civil rights movement.

The melody is in the alto line throughout this arrangement. Although "Follow the Drinking Gourd" is not a call-and-response song, I have echoed the rising, call-like motifs of the melody in the other voices.

The few notes in the soprano part that lie in the partial-thumb register are fairly easy to manage, since the thumb shifts happen after long notes or during rests. Sopranos must be attentive to changes between F♮ and F♯ in measure 2, and tenors must watch out for C♮s and C♯s throughout. All players must pay attention to the syncopations that occur frequently in all parts.

104. Great Big Stars - African-American spiritual
(SATB)

Offset rhythms in all parts and chromaticism in the middle voices make this short spiritual challenging and engaging. The sixteenth notes on beat one of the harmony parts in measures 7–10 should be played lightly and very short. The air pressure behind the tongue should be enough to make the notes speak clearly. Pushing air from the lungs for every note will make them shrill and induce light-headedness. As in other pieces with frequent rests, students should not breath at every rest, but only when needed and at musically appropriate spots.

The slurred sixteenth notes in measures 3 and 4 of the bass part can be played with the trill fingering for E♮: T/O23/OOOO. This will sound better than moving fingers 1 and 2 in opposite directions at the same time.

The lyrics are as follows:
Great big stars, \ way up– yonder, \ great big stars, \ way up– yonder, \ great big stars, \ way up– yonder; \ Oh my little soul's gonna \ shine, shine, \ oh my little soul's gonna \ shine, shine.

Star in the east, \ way up– yonder, \ star in the east, \ way up– yonder, \ star in the east, \way up– yonder; \ All around the world gonna \ shine, shine, \ all around the world gonna \ shine, shine.

The phrase "star in the east" makes it clear that this is a Christmas song, though if a holiday connection is not desired, one can sing only the first verse.

105. Michael, Row the Boat Ashore - African-American spiritual
(SATB; SAT; SAA; SAAB)

This song originated among enslaved Black people on the island of St Helena off the coast of South Carolina. It was first published in 1867 in *Slave Songs of the United States*, the first collection of spirituals ever published. In the 1950s it became a standard of the civil rights movement, and in 1961 a recording of the song by The Highwaymen was Number 1 on the hit parade.

"Michael, Row" is one of those songs that almost everyone knows and no two people sing alike. Although the tune is largely consistent, there is wide variety when it comes to lyrics. The most familiar are those sung by The Highwaymen, and they are quite different from the original.

In this arrangement, the melody is heard first in the soprano line, then in the alto line. Students playing tenor need to be careful; the notes for the second "verse" are almost the same as the first, but they are different enough that those who play by rote are likely to play notes that do not harmonize well.

106. Watah Come a Me Eye - Jamaican folk song
(SATB; SAT)

My first encounter with this lively Caribbean song was hearing a group of elementary-school students performing its refrain on steel drums. Its rhythmic vitality was striking, and the tune was stuck in my ear from that day forward. The song is in Jamaican Patois, a creole language. I have included the lyrics here even though they have no specific curricular connection, just because the song is so much fun.

*Every time I \ 'membah Liza, \ Watah come a me \ eye. \ When I think 'bout \ my girl Liza, \ Watah come a me \ eye. *
Come back, Liza, \ come back girl. \ Watah come a me \ eye. \ Come back, Liza, \ come back girl. \ Watah come a me \ eye.

To fit the definition of *creole*, a language must meet certain criteria: Creole languages are derived from multiple parent languages; they have a consistent vocabulary and consistent syntax; they are learned by children as their native tongue; and they developed in relatively recent times. It is important to note that the term *creole* is not pejorative. There are many creole languages spoken in the Western Hemisphere. Questions sometimes arise around singing with creole lyrics. Is it cultural appropriation? Is it disparaging of the people who speak it? I think that the answer to these questions is "no," unless the use of creole is done in a satirical or mocking way. In fact, I think that changing the creole language to "standard English" implies that it is not a real language or that it needs to be corrected.

The 3–3–2 rhythm that occurs in measure 3 and analogous places is a pattern called a *cinquillo*. It originated in sub-Saharan Africa and came to the Americas with enslaved Africans. It and similar patterns are found in much Latin American music. A cinquillo looks and can be counted like a syncopation. The difference is that when playing a syncopation, one feels the beats as being steady and the notes as falling between the beats, whereas in a cinquillo one feels three beats of unequal length.

The alto and bass parts in this arrangement are more challenging than the soprano and tenor parts. The C♯s in alto and bass require partial-hole fingerings, and the eighth-note figures in measures 4, 10, and 14 of the bass part will need some extra attention.

107. Ben Venga il Pastor Mio
Maddalena Casulana (c. 1544-c. 1590)
(SATB)

Maddalena Casulana was the first woman in western music history to publish an entire book of her own music. This was her *First Book of Madrigals* (*Il primo libro di madrigali*), published in 1568. Her *Second Book of Madrigals*, which includes "Ben Venga il Pastor Mio," was published in 1570. Little is known about Casulana's life. That she dedicated some of her music to Isabella de'Medici suggests possible patronage by wealthy and powerful nobles, and it is known that other prominent composers of the time held her music in high regard.

"Ben Venga il Pastor Mio" is a challenging piece, not least because of its different sound. The music is focused more on the shifting of harmonies and interplay between voices than on a distinct melody. Many of the "rules" of tonality that would become the foundation of western music did not exist in Casulana's time, and many of her harmonies may sound wrong to students accustomed to the music of later periods.

The tenor part is the most difficult from the standpoint of playing technique. It goes high into the partial-thumb register, it is quite chromatic, and there are two quick sixteenth-note figures that are difficult.

The brief shift to 3/2 time toward the end of "Ben Venga" is a device Casulana employs in several of her madrigals. The half note remains constant. It is not a difficult transition as long as students remain attentive. For that matter, there is no part of this piece which does not require attentiveness, especially with regard to rhythm and counting.

108. Un Canadien Errant - French-Canadian folk song
(SATB)

This beautiful and evocative folk melody was included in Volume 2 of this series, but its association with socio-political rebellion makes it useful in the study of modern history. Plus, the melody's simplicity lends itself to lush, expressive harmonization. The main challenge in playing it is breath control. The long phrases require plenty of air, and ideally, breaths should not be taken more often than every four measures. Students should use "belly breathing" which employs the diaphragm muscles. Often students push out the chest thinking that this gives them a deeper breath, but in reality it is the abdomen which must push forward. There is one low C in the tenor part that may be difficult for some students to play. The other parts lie in a comfortable range.

In 1837–1838, rebellions against the colonial governments of Upper and Lower Canada (in today's Ontario and Quebec) resulted in many Canadians being executed or exiled. Four years later, French-Canadian poet and novelist Antoine Gérin-Lajoie wrote lyrics to be sung to a traditional French folk song. The poem, "Un Canadien Errant" ("A Wandering Canadian"), is about the sorrow felt by Canadians who would never again be able to see their homeland.

The lyrics of the first verse are *Un Canadien er-\rant, \ banni de ses fo-\yers;\ Un Canadien er-\rant,\ banni de ses fo-\yers*
Second section: *Parcourait en pleu-\rant \ des pa-ys étran-\gers. Parcourait en pleu-\rant\ des pa-ys étran-\gers.*

109. Galliarde, from Terpsichore - Renaissance era dance tune
(SATB; SAB; SA)

The word *galliard* goes far back in English history. Geoffrey Chaucer (c. 1342–1400) used it to describe the cook in *The Canterbury Tales*: "Gaillard he was as goldfinch in the shawe" (lively he was, as a goldfinch in the woods). Like the cook, the dance is lively and energetic, involving leaps, hops and even scissor kicks.

Queen Elizabeth I of England particularly enjoyed the galliard. Even in her fifties the queen reportedly danced several galliards every morning for exercise.

Shakespeare speaks of the galliard in Act I, Scene 3 of *Twelfth Night*:
 Sir Toby: What is thy excellence in a galliard, knight?
 Sir Andrew: Faith, I can cut a caper.[30]

and later,
 Sir Toby: I did think, by the excellent constitution of thy leg,
  it was formed under the star of a galliard.

The dance is also referenced in *Henry V*, Act I Scene 2, when an ambassador says, "There's nought in France that can be with a nimble galliard won."

This particular galliard (spelled in *Terpsichore* as "galliarde") is marked "incerti," which indicates that Praetorius did not write the melody or bass line, but only filled in the harmony. I have transposed the music up a step and modified the lower voices somewhat to facilitate playing by students. There are some jumps to high notes in the soprano and alto parts that are challenging.

Michael Praetorius published *Terpsichore*, named after the Greek muse of dance, in 1612. It is a collection of over 300 dance tunes, mostly from France. Though he is generally listed as the composer, most of the dances were collected rather than composed, and Praetorius arranged them for groups of 4 to 5 unspecified instruments. See #96, "Es Ist Ein' Ros' Entsprungen," for more information on Praetorius.

---

[30] A caper is a leaping step found in many English folk dances. The word comes from the Italian "capriolare" meaning "to jump in the air." Later the word came to also mean either a playful action or a prank, hence the pun.

110. La Jesusita - Mexican folk song
(SAT with optional B)

"La Jesusita" is a song from the time of the Mexican Revolution. It originated in central Mexico, but quickly became popular throughout the country. It is a love song, but not the slow, sentimental kind. A young man asks his sweetheart to go to a dance with him; there she will see the lights, hear the happy music, and hear his words of love. The music is accordingly dancelike and cheerful.

The upper three voices jump quite a bit, making some of the fingerings difficult. The melody switches to the tenor in the refrain. The bass line is quite simple except for the need to find all of the keys for the low F♮s. The arrangement can be played with just soprano, alto and tenor. The bass part, however, brings out the harmonic rhythm of the piece.

111. Sit Down, Brother - African-American spiritual
(SATB)

Like many spirituals, "Sit Down, Brother" addresses the hardships inherent in the life of an enslaved person:

Sit down, brother,\ sit down. \ Sit down, brother, \ sit down. \ Sit down, brother, \ sit down brother, \ sit down, rest a little \ while.

Subsequent verses have lyrics such as *know you're weary, you came through lightning, you came through thunder,* and *know you had a hard time.* To sing these verses the rhythms need to be adjusted.

The bass part in this arrangement is the most challenging; students may be unfamiliar with the fingering for the A♯ in measure 2, and the G–G♯–B sequence near the end requires finger 6 to move between one and two keys. The eighth-note figure in measure 4 of the tenor part is similarly tricky, but using the trill fingering for E♯ (T/123/4O6O) makes it much easier and heightens the harmonic inflection of the E♯.

112. Strike the Bell (Click Go the Shears)
pumping shanty/bush ballad;
melody attrib. Henry Clay Work (1832-1884)
(SATB)

"Strike the Bell" is a classic example of musical borrowing. It is based on an 1865 song, "Ring the Bell Watchman," by Henry Clay Work, which was itself based on the popular "Battle Hymn of the Republic." Work's variant was later fitted with new words to become a sea shanty, "Strike the Bell," which was in turn made into an Australian bush ballad about sheep shearing. Later still, the tune was modified and given new lyrics to become a song of the temperance movement, "Sign the Pledge, Brother."

The lyrics for "Strike the Bell" focus on a ship's crew facing an approaching storm, wishing the second mate would ring the bell to send them below:

Aft on the quartet deck, walking about
There is the second mate so steady and so stout;
He is thinking of his sweetheart and he's hoping she is well;
We wish that old second mate would strike, strike the bell.

(refrain, sung after every verse):
Strike the bell, second mate, let's go below,
Look out to wind'ard, you can see it's gonna blow.
Look at the glass, you can see that it has fell,
We wish that you would hurry up and strike, strike the bell.

For'ard on the foc's'le head and keepin' sharp lookout,
There is Johnny waiting, ready fer to shout,
"Lights burnin' bright, sir, and everything is well!"
But he's wishin' that old second mate would strike, strike the bell. (refrain)

Down on the main deck, and workin' at the pumps,
There is the larboard watch ready for their bunks;
Over to wind'ard they see a great swell,
And they're wishin' that old second mate would strike, strike the bell. (refrain)

Aft at the wheel poor Anderson stands,
Graspin' the spokes in his cold-smitten hands.
Lookin' at the compass and the course is clear as hell
But he's wishin' that old second mate would strike, strike the bell. (refrain)

Aft on the quarter deck our gallant captain stands,
Lookin' to wind'ard with the glasses in his hand.
What he is thinkin' of we know very well,
He's thinkin' more of shortenin' sail than strike, strike the bell. (refrain)

Throughout the song, the given lyrics do not consistently align with the tune, and some rhythmic and melodic adjustments are needed if the song is sung.

Selected verses from the Australian version are next. It was originally called "The Bare Bellied Ewe." Again, adjustments to melody and rhythm are needed for singing.

Oh, down in the catching pen an old shearer stands,
Grasping his shears in his long bony hands;
Fixed is his gaze on a bare bellied ewe,[31]
Saying, "If I can only get her, won't I make the ringer go."[32]

(refrain, sung after every verse):
Click goes his shears; click, click, click.
Wide are the blows, and his hand is moving quick,
The ringer looks round, for he lost it by a blow,
And he curses that old shearer with the bare bellied ewe.[33]

At the end of the board, in a cane-bottomed chair,
The boss remains seated with his eyes everywhere;
He marks well each fleece as it comes to the screen,
And he watches where it comes from if not taken off clean. (refrain)

The tar boy[34] *is there, awaiting all demands,*
With his black tarry stick, in his black tarry hands.
He sees an old ewe, with a cut upon the back,
He hears what he supposes is, "Tar here, Jack." (refrain)

"Tar on the back, Jack; Tar, boy, tar."
Tar from the middle to both ends of the board.
Jack jumps around, for he has no time to sleep,
And tars the shearer's backs as well as the sheep. (refrain)

So now the shearing's over, each man has got his cheque,
The hut is as dull as the dullest old wreck;
Where was many a noise and bustle only a few hours before,
Now you can hear it plainly if a pin fall on the floor. (refrain)

Other than having quick dotted rhythms that must be steady and synchronized, "Strike the Bell" is fairly straightforward. The C–B–C figure in beats 3 and 4 of measure 11 in the soprano part can be facilitated by using the trill fingering for B♮ (T/O23/OOOO).

---

31 In the Australian outback in the 19th century, "ewe" was pronounced and sometimes spelled "yoe."

32 The ringer was the fastest shearer in the shearing shed.

33 An apparent reference to a contest or rivalry between the "old shearer" and the ringer.

34 Shearers tried to work as fast as possible, resulting in frequent cuts to a sheep's skin. The tar boy's job was to staunch the bleeding by smearing tar over the cut.

113. Ballet des Matelotz - from Terpsichore
Michael Praetorius (1571-1621)
(SATB)

"Ballet des Matelotz" (dance of the sailors) requires quick fingers and light, fast tonguing from all players. Measures 10 and 11 in the soprano part are challenging; the D–B–D figure leading from measure 10 into measure 11 is most easily played by using the trill fingering for B♮ (T/O23/OOOO). Players of all parts must be very attentive to rhythm. In particular, the tied note between measures 9 and 10 is easy to miscount.

Michael Praetorius published *Terpsichore*, named after the Greek muse of dance, in 1612. It is a collection of over 300 dance tunes, mostly from France. Though he is generally credited as the composer, most if not all of the dances under his name were collected rather than composed, and Praetorius arranged them for groups of 4 to 5 unspecified instruments.

See #96, "Es Ist Ein' Ros' Entsprungen," for biographical information about Michael Praetorius.

114. Vous, Saints Ministres du Seigneur (Old 100th)
(from the Genevan Psalter, 1539) - melody by Louis Bourgeois
(c. 1510-1561); harmonized by Claude Le Jeune (c. 1528-1600)
(SATB)

Though originally associated with the text of Psalm 134, this hymn is often called "Old 100th" because it was used in the Anglo-Genevan Psalter of 1561 to sing a translation of the hundredth psalm, "All people that on Earth do dwell." It is used to sing the Doxology in many Protestant churches ("Praise God, from Whom all blessings flow") and many other religious texts, and it is one of the best known Christian hymns. It has been quoted and paraphrased by many classical composers, from the seventeenth through twentieth centuries.

See #91, "Lass Dein' Engel mit Mir Fahren," for information on Louis Bourgeois and the Genevan Psalter.

Like Bourgeois, Claude Le Jeune was a prominent and influential composer of the 16th century. A Protestant, he composed 347 psalm settings, 38 sacred chansons, 11 motets, and a mass. During his lifetime, however, he was most celebrated for his secular songs and madrigals.

In his harmonization of the hymn, Le Jeune put the melody in the tenor, which was standard practice in his time. I have transposed the music to B♭ Major for recorders. While this puts the alto into a rather high register, it keeps the tenor in its strong range. Soprano and bass likewise move into the partial-thumb register, and the bass part has a few E♭s, a note with notoriously inconsistent intonation on bass recorders. The standard alto fingering of T/1O3/4OOO works on some bass instruments, while on others the fingering T/1O3/O56O is better. Depending on the make of your bass instruments, you may have to experiment to find a fingering that is satisfactory.

115. Leto Leta Concio - Latin round, mid-12th century
(any combination of S, A, and T, with B)

"Leto Leta Concio" is found in the 12th-century *Hortus Deliciarum*, and is one of two canons in that collection. These two are considered to be the oldest examples of canonic writing in Europe.

(1)*Leto \ leta\ conci-\o, \ haec \ di-\e, \ (2) reso-\net tri-\pudi-\o \ gra-\ti- -\e, \ (3) hoc in \ nata-\li–ti-\o \vox \ son-\net, \ (4) ortum \ dat rex \ glori-\e–\ ve-\ ni–\e.*

The text of the final two parts, *This voice will ring at the birth, the King gives rise to the coming glory*, suggests that "Leto Leta Concio" is a Christmas song. It certainly has a suitably celebratory character.

Hortus Deliciarum was written or compiled by Herrad of Landsberg (c. 1130–1195), the abbess of Hohenburg Abbey in the Alsatian region of France. It included the earliest known collection of polyphony originating in an abbey, and also included information about other artistic and academic disciplines. *Hortus Deliciarum*, which means "garden of delights" was created around 1180 for the edification of nuns in Herrad's order. Sadly, the original copy was destroyed in 1870 during the Seige of Strasbourg.

"Leto Leta Concio" was transcribed by French musicologist Yvonne Rokseth (1890–1948) from a copy of *Hortus Deliciarum*. Rokseth was not only a musician, but was active in the French Resistance during WWII. She hid Jewish students in her apartment, distributed pamphlets for the Resistance, and allowed radio broadcasts to be made from her apartment.

As written here, the melody is fairly comfortable played on the alto and extends into the partial-thumb register for soprano and tenor. I have written out the first three voices for treble clef instruments, and the fourth for bass, but in fact any voice can be played on any instrument. To play the fourth line on soprano, alto, or tenor, students can read the top line, delaying the entrance until measure 23. Similarly, any of the top three voices can be played on bass by having the students read the bass part and enter earlier. In either scenario, the students playing the changed part will need to keep track of where they need to stop. The round can also be played with two or three voices rather than four. There are a few note clashes that occur when the round is played in parts, but not more than are heard in other polyphonic music of the 12th century. The seven-bar phrases can be difficult for students who play by ear or for those who slip easily into the lulling pattern of eight-bar phrases.

116. El Vito - Andalusian folk song
(SATB; SAT)

"El Vito" dates back to the 16th century, and is a dance tune from the Andalusian region of Spain. The title refers to St Vitus, the patron saint of dancers. It is written in the Phrygian mode, with half steps between the first and second scale degrees and also between the fifth and sixth (E-F-G-A-B-C-D-E). "El Vito" frequently uses the raised third of G♯, especially when the melody rises. This gives the tune a feeling of alternating between A minor and E Phrygian. The near juxtaposition of G♯ and F♮ gives the music an other-worldly character and also makes it fairly difficult to play on C recorders. In the second section, the melody is shared by soprano and tenor. The music is also full of hemiolas, which can make it difficult to count.

117. Dalekaya i Blizkaya - Ukranian folk song
(SATB; SAT; ST; SA)

The title of this Ukranian song means "over the distant lonely mountains," but far from being reflective or melancholy, it is energetic and light-hearted.

The low D♯s in the soprano and tenor parts require the partial-hole setting of finger 6, and this can be difficult at a lively tempo. The D♯s in the alto part can be played with the trill fingering (T/1O3/OOOO). The bass part is fairly straightforward and good for students who are just getting familiar with the instrument.

118. Andalla - from 2 Moorish Tone-Pictures, Op. 19
Samuel Coleridge-Taylor (1875-1912)
(SATB)

British composer Samuel Coleridge-Taylor was the son of an English mother and a Sierra Leonean father. He was named Samuel Coleridge Taylor after the poet, Samuel Taylor Coleridge. He later hyphenated his name. His immediate family called him "Coleridge."

Coleridge-Taylor's first musical education was from his maternal grandfather, who played the violin. When it became apparent that young Coleridge had exceptional talents, his grandfather paid for him to have lessons with a professional, and at age 15 he was accepted into the Royal College of Music.

By the time he was 20, Coleridge-Taylor was gaining recognition as a gifted composer. In 1898, he composed a cantata entitled *Hiawatha's Wedding Feast* based on the epic poem by Henry Wadsworth Longfellow. The cantata was immediately popular. His exposure to American literature sparked an interest in African-American culture, furthered by the fact that his father, Daniel Taylor, was descended from Black Loyalists who had resettled in Sierra Leone.[35]

In 1899, Coleridge-Taylor married a fellow music student, Jessie Walmisley. Her parents objected to the marriage because he was of mixed race. The couple had two children: a son whom they named Hiawatha, and a daughter named Gwendolyn. Both became musicians, Hiawatha later adapting many of his father's compositions, and Gwendolyn becoming a successful composer and conductor using the professional name of Avril Coleridge-Taylor.[36]

Coleridge-Taylor never met the Bohemian composer Antonin Dvořák (Largo, from Symphony No. 8; #152), but he was impressed and inspired by Dvořák's use of traditional musical forms from his homeland in his classical compositions. He also collaborated with the African-American poet Paul Laurence Dunbar, who encouraged Coleridge-Taylor to look into the musical traditions of Sierra Leone and other parts of Africa. He did, and he became so steeped in African music that in 1925 the Sierra Leonean composer and ethnomusicologist Nicholas G. J. Ballanta wrote, "the late Mr. Coleridge-Taylor was never in Africa, yet it is interesting to see his mastery of African rhythmic forms."[37]

Coleridge-Taylor's most popular composition, *Hiawatha's Wedding Feast*, was hugely successful, selling hundreds of thousands of copies. Unfortunately for the composer, he had sold the rights to the cantata for a small amount, being (as were many composers) desperate for cash. Despite his renown as a composer and conductor, he faced financial difficulties for his entire life.

2 Moorish Tone Pictures is very much in the style of late 19th century romanticism. The inspiration behind these pieces seems to be the English translation of a

---

[35] During the American Revolution, one of Britain's strategies was to offer freedom to enslaved Black men if they would join the British army. Many of these "Black Loyalists" were resettled in Sierra Leone, which at that time was a British colony.

[36] Avril Coleridge-Taylor experienced her own travails with racial prejudice. In 1952 she was invited to tour South Africa, but when the apartheid South African government learned that her father was bi-racial, her engagements were canceled.

[37] Nicholas George Julius Ballanta (-Taylor), St Helena Island Spirituals, G. Schirmer, Inc., New York, 1925.

Spanish romance called "The Bridal of Andalla." In the poem, a maiden named Xarifa is exhorted to go to her window to see the gallant cavalier Andalla come to claim his bride. Instead, she holds back, as she is (unknown to her companions) his jilted "ex." The full ballad can be read online at https://dvpp.uvic.ca/poems/blackwoods/1820/pom_7837_andallas_bridal.html.

I have arranged the first section of Coleridge-Taylor's piece here, omitting some ornaments that would be too difficult for any but the most accomplished players. Even so, "Andalla" is challenging to play well. The alto part has some particularly tricky fingering changes.

119. Daylight: A Musical Expression
Thomas Wiggins (1849-1908)
(SATB)

Thomas Wiggins was born to an enslaved couple, Charity and Domingo Wiggins, on a Georgia plantation. In 1850 he and his parents were sold to a plantation owner, General James Bethune, who was a lawyer and a leading advocate of secession. Wiggins' name at birth was recorded as Thomas Greene, and later he was variously known as Thomas Wiggins, Thomas Greene Bethune, or Thomas Bethune, it being a common practice of the time for slaves to be identified by the family name of their enslaver.

Blind from birth, Wiggins was unable to perform the tasks typically required of the enslaved. Largely ignored, he was allowed to meander around the plantation and near the main house, where he heard Bethune's daughters playing the piano. Given access to the instrument, he was soon able to play by ear many tunes he had heard and by the age of five had composed quite elaborate pieces for the piano.

Bethune, recognizing Wiggins' extraordinary talent (and undoubtedly seeing the prospect of himself profiting from it), allowed the young boy to live in a small room off the main house which had been provided with a piano. Wiggins had an audiographic memory that enabled him to reproduce accurately any sound he heard, whether with his voice or on the piano (at which he could be found at any hour of the day). At the age of four, Wiggins was able to repeat word for word any conversation he heard, yet his ability to use language to express himself was severely limited. Descriptions of his behavior and disabilities are consistent with those which today would be diagnosed as autism. After the Emancipation Proclamation, Bethune became Wiggins' legal guardian, but Wiggins' situation changed little, if at all. He was still, for all intents and purposes, Bethune's property.

Bethune hired out Wiggins to an impresario named Perry Oliver.[38] Billing him as "Blind Tom," Oliver took Wiggins on tour, often performing several times a day. Wiggins' performances brought in the equivalent of well over a million dollars a year, money which enriched not the performer, but his managers. Adding insult to injury, Oliver publicly compared Wiggins to P.T. Barnum's "freak show," promoting him as an animal who had risen in stature to be an artist. Newspapers often compared him to a trained bear or an ape, and he was called an idiot and insane. Throughout Wiggins' life, members of the Bethune family battled over his custody.

Wiggins often referred to himself in the third person as "Tom." The cover page of the first publication of *Daylight* has the inscription, "Tom will now play for you his idea of daylight." Since the words appear as a quote, it seems likely that these may be Wiggins' own words spoken to introduce the music.

Wiggins' compositional style was the salon music that was popular among white Americans of the time, this being the genre to which he was exposed. The jazz and ragtime styles that began to emerge during his lifetime, and which were derived from African-American plantation songs, remained foreign to him. It was because Wiggins was exploited by his white managers and created music to please southern white audiences that many Black newspapers refused to acknowledge him. Particularly scorned was one of his most popular compositions, *The Battle of Manassas* (published in 1894), which commemorated the Confederate victory at Bull Run. Given Wiggins' medical status and the relative isolation in which he was kept, it seems likely that *Manassas* could have been written at the instruction of Bethune or Oliver (sensing, no doubt, that it would be a hit among southern white audiences), and that Wiggins might not have had any idea of the political implications of the piece.

During his life, Wiggins learned or wrote as many as 7,000 pieces of music. He continued to be exploited by his managers and those who held him as a ward, earning them great wealth while receiving none himself. He died of a stroke in 1909 at the age of 57.

Daylight is typical of mid- to late-19th-century American parlor music. It is full of secondary dominant harmonies and suspensions, sentimental in mood. I have arranged only the first theme for this collection, other sections of the piece being too pianistic to play on recorders. There is no tempo marking, but the harmonic rhythm suggests that it should be played on the slow side. The C♯s and low F♯s in the alto part require deft fingers, and all three parts have some wide intervals.

---

38 It was common for plantation owners to "hire out" slaves who had a unique or essential skill. Fees paid rarely benefitted the worker, going instead to the enslaver.

120. Clair de Lune - Claude Debussy (1862-1918)
(SATB)

"Clair de Lune" (moonlight) is from Debussy's *Suite Bergamasque*, published in 1905. It is one of the composer's most recognized pieces, and it is also one of the best known works in the piano repertory. Debussy's use of subtly dissonant harmonies, suspensions, and mixing of duplet and triplet rhythms all work together to create a musical impression of shimmering and shifting light.

The principle melodic material in this setting is distributed among soprano, alto, and tenor parts. The alto part is the most difficult. There are several partial-hole fingerings, and the melody in measure 7 crosses the register break, yet must be played lyrically. The soprano line also crosses the register break in multiple places that must be played smoothly. There are several places in the soprano and alto parts where notes tie across a beat or bar line. These, together with frequent shifts between duplets and triplets, make the upper voices musically challenging.

121. Oh, Watch the Stars - African-American spiritual
(SATB)

This is another spiritual from St Helena Island (see also #105, "Michael Row the Boat Ashore"). There are some tricky fingerings in the middle voices, and the shifting rhythms are challenging.

The lyrics are simple: *Oh, \ watch the stars, see how they \ run. Oh, \ watch the stars, see how they \ run. The– \ stars run down at the \ setting of the sun. Oh, \ watch the stars, see how they \ run.* Other verses about the moon and the wind have been added by folk music groups.

122. La Raspa - Mexican dance tune
(SATB)

This popular tune is used in a few different dances, including the Mexican Hat Dance. It originated in Veracruz, which is situated along the coast of the Gulf of Mexico, and it is a standard of the Mariachi repertoire.

In this arrangement, the melody is distributed among the three upper voices, while the bass provides a harmonic underpinning that is characteristic of much Mexican folk music. The B–A♯ figure in measure 15 of the alto part is easiest played with the trill fingering for the A♯ (T/123/4O6O). This also heightens the harmonic inflection of the lower neighbor. The A–G♯ figure that appears four bars later is easier, despite using the partial-hole setting of finger 6. Although in previous volumes I encouraged students to take advantage of rests to catch a quick breath, in the bass part the rests are there to achieve short, crisp articulation, and students should not breathe after every beat. The triplet figures in the bass part during the third section of the piece are also tricky. The tonguing must be done lightly, using a single exhalation on all of the notes in the group rather than blowing air separately for each individual note.

123. Joy and Thanksgiving after the Storm
from Symphony No. 6 in F Major, "Pastorale"
Ludwig van Beethoven (1770-1827)
(SATB)

Beethoven did not often engage in programatic writing, and the *Pastorale Symphony* is unique among his symphonies for this reason. Still, the composer himself indicated that the music was more of an expression of feelings than an attempt to portray scenes. Symphony No. 6 was written concurrently with Symphony No. 5, and both were premiered in the same concert (four hours in length!) on December 22, 1808. These works mark the first use of trombones in a symphony.[39]

Beethoven gave each movement of the Pastorale Symphony a programatic title, the last two being "Gewitter, Sturm" (thunderstorm, storm) and "Hirtengesang. Frohe und dankbare Gefühle nach dem Sturm" (shepherds' song. glad and thankful feelings after the storm). I have used the main theme of the finale and some of the more lightly orchestrated variations for this arrangement. The parts lie entirely in the lower register, and all require the use of finger 7. Frequent jumps in the melodies are not as difficult as one might expect, though the fingers must move in sync. The hardest spots are the "babbling brook" in measures 9–15 of the soprano part and the final scalelike passage for all four voices at the end.

124. Los Esqueletos - Costa Rican folk song
(SATB)

"Los Esqueletos" (the skeletons) is actually a children's counting song, but I have spiced it up with altered chords and deliberate dissonances to give the impression of clattering bones. The melody is heard first in the soprano, then in the bass with slight variation.

The high G♯ in measure 12 of the soprano may be unfamiliar to the students, but the fingering (Ø/12O/4OOO) is not overly difficult, and not hard to find from the preceding F♯ (Ø/123/O5OO). The G♯s in the alto part (O/O23/456O)

---

[39] Symphony No. 5 is credited with being the first, since it is Op. 67 and Symphony No. 6 is Op. 68. Given that they were composed concurrently, no one can really say whether is was the triumphant finale to No. 5 or the thunderstorm sequence in No. 6 that gave Beethoven the idea. The trombones play only in the last movement of the fifth and the last two movements of the sixth, so the trombonists had to sit for a very long time with nothing to do.

are more difficult to manage, especially when moving to or from an E (T/1OO/OOOO), as this requires the changing of every finger but No. 7. The same is true of the bass part, though all of the G♯s here are preceded or followed by A or B. All things considered, I would say alto and bass are the more difficult parts in this piece, though none of them would be considered easy for student players. Throughout the piece, players of every part must pay attention to abrupt changes between naturals and sharps.

Another challenge here is the articulation. All of the quarter notes are marked staccato, meaning that the notes are to be very short. This is accomplished by tonguing, and it is very easy for the air pressure behind the tongue to become too great and cause the notes to squawk. Adding air pressure from the lungs will almost certainly make them break. Light tonguing and controlled air flow are essential to creating a clear tone.

125. Jupiter Hymn - *from The Planets - Gustav Holst (1874-1934)*
(SATB)

Holst composed his seven movement suite *The Planets* between 1914 and 1916. He had become very interested in astrology when the idea came to him to write music that conveyed the astrological character and mood of the each planet. The suite actually has nothing to do with the planets' physical traits. Among the astrological characteristics of Jupiter are nobility and generosity, qualities which Holst sought to express in the middle section of "Jupiter," which has become known as the "Jupiter Hymn."

This piece is in the key of E♭ Major and has partial-hole and forked fingerings in all parts. In measure 11 the B♭ of the melody, being too low for soprano, is given to the alto. The hymn-like simplicity of the melody is deceptive; it is harder to play than one might expect.

126. St Agnes Eve - *third movement, excerpt*
Samuel Coleridge-Taylor (1875-1912)
(SATB)

This music comes from the *Suite from the incidental music to "St Agnes Eve,"* and the four movements are identified not with a title, but by the text spoken immediately before the music is to be played. In this case, that is "Porphyro: 'Now tell me, where is Madeline?'" I thought it simpler to just call the excerpt *St Agnes Eve.*

"The Eve of St Agnes" is a poem by John Keats (1795–1821) and is considered to be a classic example of English romantic poetry. Coleridge-Taylor's suite was written in 1912 for solo piano to accompany a tableaux presented by the Keats-

Shelley Memorial Association. Presumably the poem was read as well, since otherwise there would be no need for text cues in the music.

The biggest challenge in this piece is long phrases in a slow tempo. Ideally, breaths would be taken about every four measures, so students must learn to breathe deeply from the diaphragm (belly breathing) and not from the chest. Diaphragmatic breathing causes the abdomen, not the chest, to expand. Additional challenges are that each instrument uses most of the chromatic notes within the range of its part, and that the soprano and bass parts have wide ranges. Students must be familiar with most of the notes in the register to avoid fumbling over fingerings and disrupting the phrases.

For biographical information on Samuel Coleridge-Taylor see "Andalla" (118).

127. Hymn to the Sun - from Le Coq d'Or
Nikolai Rimsky-Korsakov (1844-1908)
(SATB; SAT)

Nikolai Rimsky-Korsakov was a member of the group of Russian composers known as "The Five" who strove to create a uniquely Russian style of classical music. He created compositions based on Russian folk songs and folk tales, and he worked in a style that favored eastern over western forms.

Initially, Rimsky-Korsakov was largely self-taught. He had gained a reputation as an exceptional orchestrator, but lacked much formal training. In 1871 he was hired to the position of Professor of Practical Composition and Instrumentation at the St Petersburg Conservatory, and he quickly realized that the gaps in his experience were impeding his teaching. At the urging of Tchaikovsky, himself a nationalist composer who had been trained in European methods, he took time off from composing to study harmony and counterpoint. This shifted his musical compositions toward a more European style, to the disapproval of the rest of The Five. Then, in 1874, Rimsky-Korsakov was asked to transcribe and arrange 140 Russian folk songs, which were published in two volumes, and also to edit the orchestral scores of ground-breaking Russian composer Mikhail Glinka (1804–1857). These projects helped him break away from the strict compositional practices he had been studying and return to developing a more personal, characteristically Russian, style.

The Russian Revolution of 1905 had relatively little immediate impact on the Russian government (though it paved the way for the 1917 revolution that deposed Tsar Nicholas II), but impacted Rimsky-Korsakov greatly. There were student demonstrations at the St Petersburg Conservatory, and when Rimsky-Korsakov openly supported the students' right to demonstrate, he was dismissed from his position. Not long after this, students staged a performance of his 1901–1902 opera *Kashchey the Deathless*. This led to another political demonstration and the banning of Rimsky-Korsakov's music. A nationwide outpouring of support for Rimsky-Korsakov came from Conservatory students and faculty, from elite intellectuals, and from peasants who had never heard his music but were outraged by the story. This, together with the appointment of a new director for the Conservatory, led to Rimsky-Korsakov being reinstated. He retired, however, in 1906.

Upon retirement, Rimsky-Korsakov began working on what would be his final opera: *Le Coq d'or,* or *The Golden Cockerel*.[40] Based on a poem by Alexander Pushkin (1799–1837), the opera became a political satire critical of Russian imperialism. The work met with opposition from government censors, and the composer's final days were spent fighting for the opera's uncensored performance. After Rimsky-Korsakov's death, the opera was finally given its Moscow premiere in 1909—with censorial edits.

The "Hymn to the Sun" is heard near the beginning of Act II and is arguably the best known portion of the opera, and it has been arranged for diverse solo instruments and ensembles.

The soprano line, sung in the opera by a coloratura soprano, is difficult to play well, both because it is highly chromatic and also because it must be smooth and sound effortless. Nevertheless, with sufficient practice it is quite manageable for experienced students. I have left out three long melismatic cadenzas which, had they been included, would have made the soprano part prohibitively hard.

The staccato eighth notes in alto and tenor are played in the opera by pizzicato strings. They should be short and light. Students should not breathe after every note, but only when necessary, making sure that the breath does not delay the following note. Ideally up to four measures would be played in a single exhalation, with the air being stopped and released by the tongue. A new exhalation on every note will result in forced tone and light-headed students. Notes longer than an eighth note in the alto and tenor parts are originally played arco by the strings, or are played by the harp (measures 13, 14, and 16).[41]

The single quarter notes on downbeats in the bass part are originally pizzicato on double basses. Play them their full value, as the low strings ring on pizzicati. The more melodic quarter notes beginning in measure 9 of the bass part are originally cellos played arco and with slurs. I have not marked slurs because the notes will not speak as clearly, but they should be played smoothly with light tonguing.

---

40 Rimsky-Korsakov's title and the libretto by Vladimir Belsky were in Russian, but the opera is best known by the French title and is often performed in French.

41 "Pizzicato" indicates that the notes are plucked. "Arco" indicates that they are played with the bow.

128. Crazy Blues - Perry Bradford (1893-1970)
(SATB)

Born in Alabama, Perry Bradford started his musical career as a young teen performing in minstrel shows. By the age of 17, he was performing as a solo pianist in Chicago and New York.

As a young musician, Bradford was exposed to the unique styles of Black American musicians and composers, and as time went by he observed that recordings of popular Black musicians tended to feature songs in the style of the white dance orchestras of the day. Convinced that there was a market for recordings of Black artists performing music from the African-American tradition, he persuaded OkeH records to record his music as sung by blues singer Mamie Smith. In 1920 "Crazy Blues" was recorded. It was a hit, selling over a million copies according to some accounts. Mamie Smith's recording of "Crazy Blues" was the first commercial recording of a blues song by a Black American singer.

Once it was evident that there was profit to be made from "race records," other recording companies began making them. Bradford continued to compose and record, and his music was widely performed by great jazz and blues musicians like Louis Armstrong. In a very real way, it was Perry Bradford (whose nickname was "Mule" owing to his stubborn nature) who paved the way for many Black musicians' careers. Rock and Roll Hall of Famer Little Richard (1932–2020) even credited Bradford with laying the groundwork for rock.

"Crazy Blues" is one of the most challenging pieces in this collection. In addition to being one of the longest, all parts have wide ranges, all are highly chromatic, and the bass line has frequent jumps of wide intervals. Blues music is often performed with swung rhythms, but in the 1920 recording Mamie Smith and her band did not use swing.[42]

129. Apart - Henry Thacker Burleigh (1866 -1949)
(SATB)

Henry (Harry) Thacker Burleigh was a Black American composer and singer who greatly influenced the art song genre in the United States.

Burleigh was a descendent of slaves. His grandfather had purchased manumission from slavery in 1833 for $55 ($50 for himself and $5 for his wife). He had moved from Maryland to Ithaca, New York, and later to Erie, Pennsylvania, where

---

[42] In jazz and some other popular music styles, swing refers to the stretching of the first of a pair of eighth notes while the second of the pair is comparably shortened. "Light swing" is less uneven than a quarter/eighth triplet, while "heavy swing" may be as uneven as a dotted rhythm. Swing rhythms should never sound calculated!

Burleigh was born in 1866. His mother, Elizabeth, was his first music teacher. She had received a degree from Avery College in 1855 and was denied a teaching position in the Erie public schools on account of her race.[43] It was she and her father who taught Burleigh the spirituals that would become central to his creative output in later years. She taught at a "colored school" in Erie.

In addition to teaching, Burleigh's mother sometimes worked as a maid for Elizabeth Russell, the daughter of his father's employer. Elizabeth Russell was a music enthusiast and socialite, and she often hosted salon concerts in her home. These concerts were segregated, Black people not being permitted to attend. When Burleigh was a teenager, he wanted so badly to hear one of these concerts that he stood outside the window of the Russells' home in freezing cold and snow to listen. Becoming sick, he admitted to his mother what he had done. She, knowing that nothing would stop her son from repeating the adventure, asked Russell to hire him as a doorman, thus enabling him to hear performances by a wide range of artists.

In 1892 Burleigh received a scholarship to attend the National Conservatory of Music. While there, his singing of spirituals caught the attention of Antonín Dvořák (Largo, from *Symphony No. 8*; #152), the Bohemian composer who had just become the director of the Conservatory. Dvořák asked Burleigh to sing for him as many spirituals and slave songs as he could remember, and he drew inspiration for many of his own compositions from Burleigh's singing. In turn, Dvořák encouraged Burleigh to preserve his own musical heritage by incorporating spirituals into his compositions. Burleigh would go on to arrange hundreds of spirituals for voice and piano and to compose many art songs that helped shape the American expression of the genre. His works were immensely popular in the 1910s and 1920s and were performed by almost every vocal recitalist in the country. It is said that Dvořák changed the instrumentation of the famous spiritual-like solo in his eighth symphony, *From The New World*, from clarinet to English horn because the latter instrument reminded him of Burleigh's singing voice.

Burleigh's compositional style was unique. Though not a jazz musician, he often used or created simple melodies and gave them highly chromatic harmonizations that would become hallmarks of the jazz idiom. "Apart," published in 1905, is characteristic of his technique. The vocal part (which appears in the soprano recorder line where it is marked "melody") has only two chromatic notes (A♯ in measure 8 and G♯ in measure 24), neither of which would be particularly out of the ordinary, but in the accompaniment scarcely a measure goes by without an altered chord or suspension. This creates an expressive richness of harmony while maintaining the folk-like simplicity of a mostly diatonic melody.

---

[43] Avery College, which operated in Pittsburgh, PA, from 1849 to 1873, was the first college in the U.S. to offer higher education to Black Americans.

Nearly 2,000 people attended Burleigh's funeral at St George's Episcopal Church in New York City, where he had sung as a soloist for over 50 years. Ironically, when Burleigh was hired at St George's in 1894, many of the congregation had objected strenuously to having a Black cantor in the church.

130. It Was a Lover and His Lass - Thomas Morley (1557-1602)
(SATB)

The 1588 publication of a collection of Italian madrigals called *Musica Transalpina* seems to have been the inspiration for Thomas Morley to begin writing English madrigals which blended the Italian form with the English compositional style. During his lifetime, Morley was one of the best-known composers of secular music in England, and he was a leading figure of the English madrigal school. Morley's madrigals tend to be light in character and readily singable, a marked change from the Italian school. He also wrote purely instrumental music. Many of his keyboard arrangements of English folk tunes are found in the Fitzwilliam Virginal Book, and he was one of the first composers to write for "broken" consorts.[44] In 1592 Morley was given the title of "Gentleman of the Chapel Royal." His *Plaine and Easie Introduction to Practicall Musicke* was published in 1597 and is an important source of information about music and performance practices of the 16th century.

"It Was a Lover and His Lass" is a setting of text from Shakespeare's *As You Like It*, and was first published in Morley's *Ayres or Little Short Songs, Book 1*, in 1600. It is not known whether Morley's setting was ever performed by Shakespeare's company, but the two men did live in London at the same time. Since *As You Like It* is believed to have been written in 1599, it remains a possibility. "It Was a Lover" is one of the few surviving musical settings of Shakespearean text from one of his contemporaries. Musically speaking, the song lies between the Renaissance and Baroque eras. The melody is in the mixolydian mode,[45] but the emphatic presence of F♯s in the middle voices and frequent root movement by fifth move the music strongly in the direction of 17th-century tonality.

As was standard for the time, Morley wrote this music without bar lines, but rather used vertical lines in the lute/vocal part to indicate phrases in the text. The alla breve marking at the beginning does not indicate that the music is in

---

[44] Throughout much of the Renaissance era, the ideal for instrumental music was the "whole" or "closed" consort, which consisted entirely of like instruments; a group of viols (often called a chest of viols) was the most popular, but consorts of recorders or other instruments were used. A "broken" or "mixed" consort used diverse instruments. A more specific grouping of three plucked strings, two bowed strings, and a recorder was popular in Elizabethan England and is referred to as either an English consort or a Morley consort.

[45] Using a major scale with a lowered seventh, in this case G–A–B–C–D–E–F♮–G.

2/2 time throughout, but rather that the half-note is the beat. There are several places where textual and musical phrasing is at odds with a strict 2/2 meter, and performers in Morley's time would have followed the text, shifting apparent meters where appropriate. Toward the end of the setting, the descending eighth-note figures (which imitate the ringing of bells) would probably have been perceived as all beginning on a strong beat, such that the implied bar lines would not have been aligned. This being inconsistent with today's notational practice, modern editions simply have the echoing figures (in the alto and tenor) straddle the bar line.

Another interesting feature of the original publication is that the two parts (one for voice and lute, the other for bass viol) are on opposite pages facing opposite directions. This allowed both musicians to sit facing one another with the music on a table, reading from the same copy.

Morley's polyphonic writing in this setting makes it challenging as an ensemble piece. Precise counting is imperative. Be particularly aware of rhythm in places where a note is tied across a bar line. The upper three voices move into the partial-thumb register, and those playing the lower three voices must be attentive to chromatic changes throughout the piece.

131. Ain't Gonna Let Nobody Turn Me Around
African-American spiritual
(SATB)

This song became prominent in American culture as a protest song of the Civil Rights movement of the 1950s and 60s. It was sung during the 1968 Memphis sanitation workers' strike as they marched in protest of the conditions faced by the mostly Black employees of the Department of Public Works. The song is based on a traditional spiritual, "Don't You Let Nobody Turn You Round."

Because of the distinctive rhythm in measures 2, 3 and 4 of the melody, I have used a rhythm pattern called a cinquillo in much of the accompaniment. The cinquillo originated in sub-Saharan Africa and came to the Americas with the slave trade. It and similar patterns are found in both African-American and Latin American music. A cinquillo looks and can be counted like a syncopation. The difference is that when playing a syncopation, one feels the beats as being steady and the notes as falling between the beats, whereas in a cinquillo one feels three beats of unequal length: 3/8–3/8–2/8.

The alto and bass parts in this arrangement are difficult. The alto part has many C♯s and B♭s, and the chromatic figures in the bass line make for challenging fingering changes. However, for a group of capable students, the piece's chromaticism and lively, offbeat rhythms make it inherently interesting.

132. Shine Like a Morning Star - U.S. folk song
(SATB)

This is one of those songs that lends itself to a variety of musical styles. I have chosen to give it a blues feel with light swing in the eighth notes. The chromaticism makes the arrangement challenging but engaging, especially for older students who are longing for something different. The low C♯s in the bass and tenor parts are difficult, but playing the music at a moderate tempo will make them easier to find.

The lyrics are simple: *Shine—, \ shine, \ shine– like a \ star in the morn–ing–, \ shine —, \ shine all a-\round the throne of \ God. (I know I'm gonna)*

133. Saint Louis Blues - W.C. Handy (1873-1958)
(SATB)

Though he is often called "Father of the Blues," William Christopher Handy did not invent the genre. Rather, he was one of the first composers to publish music in the blues style and was instrumental in popularizing the blues. Handy began his musical career at the age of 19 playing trumpet in a Birmingham, Alabama band. By age 23, he had become the bandmaster of Mahara's Colored Minstrels, touring with them for three years—a job for which he was paid $6 per week. In the early 1900s, Handy traveled extensively throughout the South, writing down the popular African-American music he heard there. This experience greatly influenced his musical style, and in 1909 he wrote "The Memphis Blues," which was his first big success. Handy also started a publishing company that printed and distributed works by Black composers.

By 1914 tango had become the most popular dance in America. Handy began his new "Saint Louis Blues" with an introduction that featured the habañera rhythm (dotted quarter/eight, quarter, quarter) before sliding into his now famous blues melody. The mix of musical styles and Handy's departure from the standard twelve-bar blues format in the introduction brought criticism from some other blues musicians.

Though successful, Handy had many struggles throughout his career. He had difficulty convincing Black musicians to perform his music, in large part because they were focused on music that white audiences enjoyed and were reluctant to take risks with a new, relatively untested style. Ironically, it was white bands, who were more sure of their audiences and could afford to be less risk-averse, that performed Handy's music the most. This was how things stood until 1920, when Perry Bradford's breakthrough recording of "Crazy Blues" (#128) brought blues into the limelight. Then, adding additional irony, Handy's own success drew others into the field, increasing the competition.

I have arranged only the first and best-known section of "Saint Louis Blues" for this collection. All of the parts are quite chromatic, and none is easy to play. The song is typically played with moderate swing—the rhythmic stretching of the first of a pair of eighth notes. Swung rhythms are not precisely like either triplets or dotted rhythms, and they should have a spontaneous feel.

134. Magnetic Rag - Scott Joplin (1868-1917)
(SATB)

For many, the name of Scott Joplin is synonymous with ragtime. And for good reason; during his lifetime he was known as "the king of ragtime." Not long after Joplin's death, ragtime was replaced by jazz as the preeminent style of popular music.

Ragtime developed in Black communities in St Louis, Missouri, in the late 19th century. Initially it was largely improvised, only being written down beginning in the 1890s. Much ragtime music was played in bars and informal settings. Joplin, however, regarded the genre as a form of classical music intended for concert performance. In addition to piano rags, he also composed a ragtime ballet and two operas, several songs, and an instruction manual called The *School of Ragtime*. His only surviving opera, *Treemonisha*, was a financial disaster for Joplin. He was unable to find a publisher, so he paid out-of-pocket to print the work in a reduced score for voices and piano. In 1915 he staged an under-rehearsed performance in Harlem for an invited audience, which included several potential backers. The production lacked any of the grandeur of European opera, and the audience, unenthused, walked out. Two years later Joplin died at the age of 48 of syphilis. His last years were plagued by dementia.

The term *ragtime* comes from the syncopated or "ragged" rhythms that are central to the style. In several of Joplin's published rags there is the statement that "ragtime is never played fast." In *The School of Ragtime*, the composer also notes that "the 'Joplin ragtime' is destroyed by careless or imperfect rendering, and very often good players lose the effect entirely, by playing too fast."[46]

In addition to syncopation, ragtime piano music is characterized by leaps in the left hand and oscillating patterns of sixteenth notes in the right hand. Both techniques are difficult or impossible to replicate on recorders. Leaps in the bass line that would go beyond the range of the bass recorder have been narrowed. I dealt with the oscillating right hand patterns by dividing the notes between two voices, one playing eighth notes on the beat, the other playing offbeats. This can be seen in the alto and tenor parts in measure 6; in the soprano and alto parts in measures 13, 15, 17, and 19; between soprano and tenor in measure 24; and between soprano and both middle voices in measure 28. For this effect to be successful, rhythmic precision is paramount.

---

46 Joplin, Scott, *School of Ragtime, 6 exercises for piano*, 1908, New York, published by Scott Joplin.

135. Solace, A Mexican Serenade - Scott Joplin (1868-1917)
(SATB)

Although the composer calls "Solace" Mexican, the rhythm in the bass is actually that of the habañera, which originated in Cuba. The writing blends the syncopated rhythms of ragtime in the upper voices with the Latin American flavor of the habañera (which is sometimes shared with the tenor) in the bass line. I have arranged only the first section of the piece here.

"Solace" should be played on the slow side, with a relaxed rather than excited feel. The short chromatic scales should glide easily to their destination.

For more information on Scott Joplin and ragtime music, see #134, Magnetic Rag.

136. Lift Every Voice and Sing
J. Rosamond Johnson (1873-1954)
(SATB)

"Lift Every Voice and Sing" is a collaboration of songwriting team J. Rosamond Johnson and James Weldon Johnson. It is a hymn with a march-like character expressing the struggles of Black Americans in the Reconstruction era. In 1919, the NAACP began referring to the song as the "Negro National Anthem." It later was referred to as the "Black National Anthem." The song was widely sung during the civil rights era.

Wide ranges, quick tonguing, and frequent chromaticism make this piece challenging to play on recorders.

For more information on J. Rosamond Johnson, see #99, "Dem Bones."

137. Charleston - James P. (Jimmy) Johnson (1894-1955)
(SATB)

"The Charleston" was the most popular dance of the Roaring Twenties, and it preexisted J.P. Johnson's 1923 song of the same title (Johnson said he had seen it danced in 1913). Nevertheless, it was Johnson's music that propelled it into the dance craze that became emblematic of the period. The dance may have its roots in the African-American dance tradition known as juba. Juba was a competitive dance in which dancers sought to outdo one another with their endurance and the complexity of their steps and rhythm. The sequence of steps associated with the dance today were first performed in the Broadway musical *Runnin' Wild* in 1923. Song and dance became immediate hits what dominated dance halls until nearly the end of the decade.

Musically the Charleston is characterized by a dotted quarter/eighth rhythm in beats 1 and 2 of every measure. This gives it an asymmetrical drive. In Johnson's song, this rhythm appears in both the melody and the accompaniment, broken occasionally by syncopated measures in straight 4/4 time. Its appeal is furthered by the chromaticism ubiquitous to the jazz era.

James (Jimmy) Price Johnson (1894–1955) was born in New Jersey and grew up listening to the ragtime music of Scott Joplin. The African-American songs he heard and sang in his youth also influenced his later style. Johnson had perfect pitch and as a child was able to play many tunes on the piano by ear. In 1912, he left school to focus his attention on developing a musical career. He studied both classical piano repertoire and the music of ragtime composers, and he began composing his own rags. Eventually he developed a unique style known as "stride piano," which greatly influenced later jazz musicians. Stride is characterized by a one-line melody in the right hand with a left-hand accompaniment that jumps from single bass line notes to thick chords an octave or more away.

The 1930s brought two things that would impact Johnson's career. First was a change in the musical tastes of the general public. The vigorous steps of the Charleston had been possible because the short dresses of the flapper style allowed free movement of the legs. Fashions change, and floor-length sheath evening dresses came into vogue. This type of apparel required that dancers move in a gliding manner completely unsuited to Johnson's music. The second was the Great Depression (1929–1939). Johnson was fortunate in that royalties from his earlier publications and recordings enabled him to survive and continue to develop his compositional style, but his applications for financial support from foundations were unsuccessful. In the late 1930s, traditional jazz became re-popularized, and Johnson was able to rejuvenate his performing and recording career.

In 1951, a severe stroke ended Johnson's playing career. His death four years later was barely noted by news organizations. Johnson was posthumously inducted into the Songwriters' Hall of Fame in 1970.

PART D - Music in Five or More Parts

The music in this section does not follow the usual SATB instrumentation. Some of the pieces are canons written for more than four voices. Many of these can be performed with fewer players by adjusting the ending. Others were composed for five or more distinct voices, and one, the Largo from Dvořák's Symphony No. 7, has such thick harmonization in the original that I felt it would be a disservice to reduce it to four parts. The initial pieces in this section are fairly easy to play, though playing them in multiple parts may be challenging. Those toward the end of the section are quite difficult.

138. Alleluia - canon in eight parts - anonymous French
(any combination of S, A, T, and B)

This round can be performed in as few as three parts. With three or four voices, it works best if entrances are spaced at two measure intervals. In this key it is most easily played on alto recorders. Played on soprano or tenor it has two notes requiring the partial-thumb setting. Ideally, there should be no breathing until the repeat sign, but if necessary a quick auxiliary breath can be taken after the half note in measure 4. The lyrics are simple: *Allelu-\ia, al-\lelu-\ia, lou-\ange mon \ dieu, al-\ lelu-\ia.*

139. Galileo's Epitaph - canon in five parts
music by Joseph Haydn (1731-1809)
(originally Der Hirsch, Hob. XXVIIb: 32)
139a. (any combination of A and B)
139b. (any combination of S and T)

Whoever first thought of singing four lines of Sarah Williams' "The Old Astronomer to His Pupil" to Haydn's canon took a few liberties. First of all, the selected lines of the poem do not fit the music; an additional line is needed, hence the repetition of "fearful of the night." Second, Haydn's canon "Der Hirsch" (the deer) is meant to be sung fast, whereas "Galileo's Epitaph" is slow and reflective. Finally, there is no indication in the poem that either the mentor or his pupil is Galileo. Nevertheless, the borrowing works.

Because of its usefulness in supporting the study of astronomy and the unpredictability of middle-school students' singing ranges, I have included the canon in two different settings: one for C instruments in D minor, and one for F instruments in G minor. The two settings should not be played together. The wide range of a minor tenth, together with the melody's flowing character, made it impractical to adjust the tune to be playable on all recorders together.

The fingerings are identical for all instruments.[47] The lyrics that fit the canon are below:

Though my soul may \ set in darkness, \ it will rise in \ perfect light–; \ I have \ loved the stars too \ fondly to be \ fearful of the \ night, fearful \ of the night.

Although I often try to adapt the end of a canon so that all voices can end together, in this case I find it more satisfying to let the voices drop out one at a time and end with the questioning nature of the unresolved diminished triad.

Sarah Williams (1837–1868) was an English writer who published her work under the pseudonyms Sadie (her childhood nickname) and S.A.D.I. "The Old Astronomer" was published after her death in a collection of poetry called *Twilight Hours: A Legacy of Verse*. The lines of the poem sung in "Galileo's Epitaph" are the most frequently quoted of her writings.

Joseph Haydn (1732–1809) was one of the titans of the Classical era of European music. He lacked the native talent of Wolfgang Mozart (who called him "Papa Haydn") and made his way musically from quite awkward, error-laden early compositions to masterpieces that remain central pillars of the classical repertoire today. He had no formal training in composition or counterpoint, teaching himself instead by studying Johann Joseph Fux's *Gradus ad Parnassum* and the works of Carl Phillipp Emanuel Bach. Haydn is often called "the father of the symphony" and "the father of the string quartet" for his ground-breaking achievements in those genres. He composed at least 104 symphonies and 67 string quartets.

The designation Hob. XXVIIb: 32 is from the catalog of Haydn's work created by Dutch musicologist Anthony van Hoboken (1887–1963). Hoboken spent some forty years working on this catalog. Much if not all of Haydn's music existed only in unpublished form at the time of his death. Rather than organizing the compositions chronologically, a near impossible task for over 750 pieces of music, Hoboken grouped them by musical genre. Category XXVII is sacred and secular canons: "a" being the designation for sacred canons, of which there are ten, and "b" being the designation for secular canons, of which there are 47.

---

47 With the exception that tuning discrepancies might make it necessary to use alternative fingerings for the E♭s in the bass part.

140. Let's Have a Peale for John Cooke's Soule
canon in eight parts from Pammelia
Thomas Ravenscroft (c. 1582-c. 1635)
(any combination of S, A, T, and B)

The top line of this round can be played by any treble clef recorder, provided altos play the parenthetical Cs. In the original, the tune drops to the low Cs. With this octave displacement, the round becomes considerably easier to play on the alto than on soprano or tenor. That said, it is better played on C instruments because the low Cs begin to sound like pealing bells. The round looks deceptively simple, but careful counting is needed for everyone to stay in the right place. It can be played or sung with fewer than eight voices, but the bell-like effect is diminished with every part omitted. One could add a low chime (on the note C) or two (on C and G) to bring out the tolling effect. This is a good way to involve students who have arm or hand injuries that prevent them from playing recorder.

Lyrics for the round are: *Let's have a \ peale for \ John Cooke's \ soul, \ for he was a \ very very honest \ man, \ an honest \ man.*

For biographical information about Ravenscroft, see #63, "Miserere Nostri Domine."

141. Laudate Nomen - canon in seven parts from Pammelia
Thomas Ravenscroft (c. 1582-c. 1635)
(any combination of S, A, T, and B)

If this canon is played as written, the various parts drop out one at a time. I find this unsatisfying for a celebratory piece, preferring a full sound at the final cadence. To accomplish this, it is necessary to adjust the notes for some voices at the end. I recommend having the bass instruments play until they return to measure 1 (C–F) and end there. Other players play the first note of whatever measure they are on, and finish the measure with an F, A, or C, to make an F Major chord.

The empty bar at the end is a bit of a conundrum. I can imagine only two reasons for it being there: 1) to allow singers to take a deep breath before starting the round again, and 2) Ravenscroft had no other rounds for seven voices to include in *Pammelia*. In any case, there are never more than six voices singing or playing at a time, so calling it a canon for seven seems a bit of a stretch.[48]

---

[48] Ravenscroft does the same thing in "Sing We Now Merrily" (#145) but indicates that it is for ten or eleven voices. In that case, the ten-voice option merely would omit the final empty beats.

The lyrics are simple: *Lauda-\te nomen \ Domi-\ni, super \ omnes \ gentes.*

For biographical information about Ravenscroft, see #63, "Miserere Nostri Domine."

142. Jubilate Deo - canon in five parts
Michael Praetorius (1571-1621)
(any combination of S, A, T, and B)

To end this canon, I have every player play a fermata on beat four of the last measure they play, with the lowest instruments ending in measure 3. Those ending with measure 4 (which has a rest on the fourth beat) can play a C or an E. Those ending with measure 2 put the fermata on the E, dropping the D at the end of the measure.

"Jubilate Deo" is quite easy to play on alto recorder. On C recorders there are frequent crossings of the register break.

Lyrics: *Jubilate, \ jubilate– Deo omnis \ terra, jubi-\late omnis terra, \ psalite in laetitia.*

For more information on Michael Praetorius see #96, "Es Ist Ein' Ros' Entsprungen."

143. Sumer Is Icumen In - canon in four parts
English, 13th century
(S or T), with T/A or B ground bass (Pes)

This is the oldest-known English language canon. Written in Middle English, its source is a manuscript dating to circa 1260 found in Reading Abbey and preserved in the British Library.

It is unclear how many voices were intended for singing this round. The manuscript has performance notes from the scribe, which indicate that the song may be sung by four, but it does not indicate whether this is a recommended number or a minimum. It does not tell us whether those four are all singing the rota (round), or if there are two on the rota and two on the pes. Some modern editions call for six voices performing the rota. Others call for four on the rota and two on the pes (ground bass). I have done it with choirs singing the rota in eight parts. It is interesting and challenging, but given the amount of note doubling it doesn't add much to the music.

The range of the rota is too wide to be comfortably played on both C and F recorders. I have kept it in the original key, to be played by C recorders. My preference is to play the rota entirely on sopranos, using altos, tenors, and/or basses on the pes, being careful not to let any voice overpower the others. I have written the pes in both treble and bass clef, but it is not necessary to use both treble and bass instruments; the parts are identical. The scribe indicates that the first voice of the rota should begin at the same time as the pes. Presumably both pes I and pes II are to intended to begin simultaneously.

The Middle English text for the rota is:
*Sumer is i-\cumen in—, \ Lhude sing cuc-\cu, *
*Groweþ sed and \ bloweþ med and \ springþ þe wde \ nu; *
*Sing cuc-\cu, *
*Awe bleteþ \ after lomb lhouþ \ after calue \ cu \ Bulluc sterteþ \ bucke uerteþ *
murie sing cuc-\cu.
Cuccu \cuccu– \ Wel singes þu \ cuccu ne \ swik þu nauer \ nu.

Text for the pes lines repeats.
Pes 1: *Sing cuccu nu–, Sing cuccu,*
Pes 2: *Sing cuccu, Sing cuccu nu–.*

Interestingly, the Reading manuscript has a second set of religious lyrics pertaining to the Crucifixion, "Perspice Christicola, que dignacio." This has caused a "chicken and the egg" (or would that be the cuckoo and the egg?) debate among early music scholars. Another hot topic of debate is whether the "bucke" that "verteth" is leaping or flatulent.

For more detailed information on the pes (ground bass) see notes to #56, "Ah Robin, Gentle Robin."

144. Joy in the Gates of Jerusalem
canon in six parts from Pammelia
Thomas Ravenscroft (c. 1582-c. 1635)
(any combination of S, A, T, and B)

This little round can be sung or played with as few as two voices. Alto players must play the parenthetical note in measure 4. The finger change between F♯ to B♭ is tricky, but otherwise the biggest challenge is not playing early in measure 5, which has a rest on beat 1.

The lyrics are: *Joy in the \ gates of \ Jeru-\salem; \ peace bee in \ Sion.* [Zion]

For biographical information about Ravenscroft, see #63, "Miserere Nostri Domine."

145. Sing We Now Merrily - round in ten parts from Pammelia
Thomas Ravenscroft (c. 1582-c. 1635)
(any combination of S, A, and T)

Because of its long phrases and lively tempo, I have arranged this piece for treble clef instruments only. In measures 2–5 and again near the end, altos must play the parenthetical notes. Ravenscroft indicates that the round is for ten or eleven voices. The tune falls into ten segments of equal length, and there are rests at the end for the entrance of an eleventh voice. I have left these out, as they make almost no change in the way the piece sounds.

Lyrics: *Sing we now \ merrily our \ purses be \ empty hey \ ho, \ let \ them take care that \ list to spare for \ I will not do \ so, \ who can \ sing so \ merry a note, \ as he that \ cannot change a \ groat, hey \ hoe trolly lolly \ loe, trolly lolly lo.*

I have made one rhythmic change toward the end: Ravenscroft wrote the word "trolly" under a single quarter note. I have made it two eighth notes instead, guessing that this was the intent.

For biographical information about Ravenscroft, see #63, "Miserere Nostri Domine."

146. Now Thanked Bee the Great God Pan
canon in six parts from Pammelia
Thomas Ravenscroft (c. 1582-c. 1635)
(any combination of S, A, T, and B)

Given the nature of its lyrics, this round might be better played rather than sung, at least when it comes to students. The "speaker" is clearly not content in her marriage.

Now \ Thank-ed \ bee the \ great God \ Pan, which \ thus– pre-\serves my \ lov-ed \ life, and \ thank-ed be \ I that \ keeps a \ man who \ end-ed \ hath this \ blondy \ strife, for \ if– my \ man must \ praises \ have, what \ then must \ I that \ keepe the \ knave.

I have no idea what is meant by "blondy strife," nor have I been able to find any source that gives a 16th century definition. My best guess would be that it is a copyist's error for "bloody." In any case, there is a negative connotation.

On C recorders the music extends into the partial-thumb register. On alto it is quite manageable, and on bass the major technical challenge is the length of the phrases. I have taken the third phrase down an octave from the original to narrow the playing range.

For biographical information about Ravenscroft, see #63, "Miserere Nostri Domine."

147. Thebana Bella - double canon in six parts
W.A. Mozart (1756-1791)
(SSSAAA)

This is a double canon: two canons that can be sung or played simultaneously. Mozart wrote it in the summer of 1770 when he was 14 years old. I have indicated for the top line to be played on sopranos and the bottom line on altos, mostly so that the difference in timbre will help differentiate the voices. Mozart wrote both parts in the same range in treble clef, so using other combinations are fine. The piece being so short, one might have the groups switch parts at the repeat. Both lines are significantly easier to play on alto than on soprano. The fingering changes between E♭ and F♮ are quite tricky on C instruments (E♭ – O/O23/456O; F♮ – Ø/123/4O6O).

148. Jinkin the Jester - canon in five parts from Pammelia
Thomas Ravenscroft (c. 1582-c. 1635)
(any combination of S, A, T, and B)

Jinkin the \ jester was \ wont to make \ glee with \ Jarius the \ juggler till \ angry was \ he, then \ Wilkin the \ Wiseman did \ wisely fore-\see, that \ Juggler and \ Jester should \ gently a-\gree, \ hey down, down, \ down, down derie \ down, down, down, down, \ down, down.

This spirited round goes into the partial-thumb register for all instruments, but is especially challenging on soprano and tenor; the high B in measure 13 was not introduced in any of the previous volumes, and the fingering (Ø/12O/45OO), while not difficult to find, will be unfamiliar. Moving from high G (Ø/123/OOOO) to high B requires only lifting finger 3 while setting fingers 4 and 5. Regulating air flow for a new fingering in the high register is always a bit of a challenge. Altos must play the parenthetical note in measure 7 in order to stay in their range.

For biographical information about Ravenscroft, see #63, "Miserere Nostri Domine."

Part D – Music in Five or More Parts

149. Now Is the Month of Maying - Thomas Morley (1557-1602)
(SSATB)

Though it is overly not hard to play, the continuously changing rhythms in the inner voices make this madrigal difficult to keep together. Those playing inner voices must also be very attentive to the abrupt chromatic shifts that are characteristic of music of the English Renaissance. The little "chasing" eighth-note figures toward the end are a favorite gesture of Morley. I have simplified the rhythm of the inner voices somewhat, replacing repeated pairs of eighth notes with a single quarter in places where the eighths are only needed for singing.

For more information on Thomas Morley and English madrigals, see the notes for #130, "It Was a Lover and His Lass."

150. Pavane 'Le Bon Vouloir' - from Danceries, Livre 4 (1550)
Claude Gervaise (1525-1583)
(SAATB)

French composer Claude Gervaise was best known for his dance music, and he also wrote a large number of chansons. However, his biggest contribution to musical history are innovations to the notation of instrumental music.

Gervaise's instrumental music is largely homophonic, making it relatively easy to play in an ensemble. His harmonies, though, sound unusual to the modern ear. "Pavane" begins as if it is going to be in the key of C, but consistently drifts into the Mixolydian mode, both of C and of G. The final cadence is to a G Major chord, but this is preceded by a minor dominant, making a G Mixolydian cadence. This kind of modal mixing, even when accompanied by what seems to be a standard tonal bass line, is common in music of the late Renaissance.

The pavane is a stately dance. In the 16th century, it was played at the beginning of courtly dances, providing an opportunity for the aristocracy to process and show off their finery. Later it was also used in churches for solemn occasions. Later still, composers like Maurice Ravel would use the dance to express sorrow.

151. Canon 8 Parts: in 4. Retro & Retro.
from A Plaine and Easie Introduction to Practicall Musicke (1597)
Thomas Morley (1557-1602)
(SSAATTBB)

This is a "riddle" or "puzzle" canon. In this type of writing, the composer gives only part of the music and perhaps offers clues for its completion. In this case, Morley gives only four parts, here labeled as S1, A1, T1, and B1. The clues are in the title: there are to be eight voices, not four, and the solution involves turning things backward.

I cannot take credit for solving the puzzle; that was done centuries ago, with some help from Morley himself. It goes like this: the second half of S1 turned backward becomes the first half of S2; the second half of A1 turned backward becomes the first half of A2; the second half of T1 turned backward becomes the first half of T2; and the second half of B1 turned backward becomes the first half of B2. This provides half of each of the four missing voices.

Next, the first half of S1 is turned backward to become the second half of S2; the first half of A1 is turned backward to become the second half of A2; the first half of T1 turned backward becomes the second half of T2; and the first half of B1 turned backward becomes the second half of B2.

I suggest a moderate tempo for playing this canon, slow enough to hear the voicing, yet fast enough to avoid running out of air. Other than the long phrases, the technical challenges are partial-thumb fingerings in the soprano parts and the use of finger 7 in tenor and bass.

For more information on Thomas Morley, see the notes for #130, "It Was a Lover and His Lass."

152. Largo - from Symphony No. 8 (From the New World) Antonin Dvořák (1841-1904)
(SATTB)

Antonín Dvořák was a Bohemian composer who successfully sought to meld the traditional music of his native land with with the forms of classical music.[49] He did this in part by integrating folk dance rhythms and structures into symphonic works, chamber music, and piano compositions. In 1877, having three times won the Austrian State Stipendium, a competition for musical composition, Dvořák attracted the attention of the famous Johannes Brahms, who recommended him to his publisher, Simrock. Although Brahms was not known for being supportive of young composers, the two became good friends. Brahms not only encouraged Dvořák, but also offered advice. It was by studying the symphonies of Brahms that Dvořák developed his mastery of orchestration. So high was Brahms' esteem for Dvořák, that, when Dvořák was in the United States, Brahms performed the menial and arduous task of proofing the plates for Dvořák's compositions before they were published by Simrock.

In 1892 Dvořák became the director of the National Conservatory of Music in New York. At that time the National Conservatory was one of the only schools

---

49 In the mid-19th century, Bohemia was part of the Austrian Empire. Today that region is within the Czech Republic.

that accepted female and Black students. Among the students at the Conservatory was a Black baritone named Henry Thacker Burleigh (129, "Apart"). Burleigh sang for Dvořák the spirituals he had learned as a child from his mother and grandfather, and Dvořák was so taken by the music that he wrote, "I am convinced that the future music of this country must be founded on what are called Negro melodies. These can be the foundation of a serious and original school of composition, to be developed in the United States. These beautiful and varied themes are the product of the soil. They are the folk songs of America and your composers must turn to them."[50]

In some ways Dvořák was correct in his prediction. Although many American composers of concert music went in the direction of the experimentalists, the genres of ragtime, blues, and jazz evolved from the old spirituals. Interestingly, later European composers, notably Maurice Ravel and Igor Stravinsky, would find inspiration in these styles and integrate elements of ragtime and jazz into their own classical compositions.

In 1893, when Dvořák was commissioned by the New York Philharmonic to compose a symphony (his eighth, given the title *From the New World*), he drew on this inspiration. Contrary to popular belief, the famous theme of the second movement is not a traditional spiritual melody, but rather was composed by Dvořák with the intent of evoking the mood of spirituals. It was in 1922 that the tune was used by William Arms Fisher, another of Dvořák's pupils, in writing the lyrics for the song "Goin' Home." It is said that Dvořák originally intended the theme to be played by a clarinet, but changed to the cor anglais (English horn) because it reminded him of Henry Burleigh's voice.[51]

Dvořák also greatly influenced the work of Black British composer Samuel Coleridge-Taylor (118, "Andalla"; #126, "St Agnes Eve"). Though they never met, Coleridge-Taylor was inspired by Dvořák's incorporation of Bohemian music into classical genres.

I have arranged this excerpt for 5 voices so that the melody need not be involved in the chorale-like music that opens and closes the movement. Of course, no instrument in the recorder family can replicate the mournful quality of the English horn, but I have kept the soprano melody in the lowest possible register to at least capture some of the melancholy character.

---

50 Gutmann, Peter. "Dvorak's *"New World"* Symphony". *Classical Classics*. Classical Notes.

51 *Cor anglais* actually means "angled horn," a reference to the bent bocal which allows the player to reach both the reed and the keys. The instrument developed in France.

I find it fascinating that Dvořák chose to bookend his simple hexatonic[52] melody with colorfully chromatic chords. The opening progression is like a musical daybreak preceding a pastoral hymn.

The challenge in playing this piece is the slow tempo coupled with long, smooth phrases. Students may be tempted to breathe after every measure, but this will disrupt the flow of the music. Breathing after every fourth measure is ideal, but may not be sustainable for younger players. Every two measures is a reasonable compromise. The students will need to learn to breathe deeply, from the diaphragm (belly breathing).

153. Sinfonia à 5 - Op. 6 No. 29 - Salamon Rossi (c. 1570-1630)
(SSATB)

This piece is from Rossi's *Il Secondo Libro Della Sinfonie, Gagliarde, e Canzoni a 3, 4 e 5* (the second book of sinfonias, gagliardes, and canzons, for 3, 4, and 5 [instruments]) published in 1608. Salamon Rossi was a Jewish violinist and composer living in Mantua, where he worked as a court musician. He was a prominent figure in the early Italian Baroque and a major innovator in the area of instrumental music. Among his published works are a range of sinfonias, dances (especially galliardes), sonatas, and Jewish liturgical music.

In the late 16th and early 17th centuries, anti-Jewish sentiments were strong in Italy as well as throughout Europe. In Mantua, Jews were required to wear yellow badges in public.[53] Rossi was so highly regarded at the Mantuan court that he was exempted from this requirement. Rossi died during the War of Mantuan Succession that followed the death of Vincenzo II, Duke of Mantua and Montferrat. The immediate cause of his death is not known, but it probably occurred when invading Austrian troops destroyed the Jewish ghetto in Mantua. It may also have been during the outbreak of plague that followed the war.

A "sinfonia" of Rossi's time has little connection to the large-scale, multi-movement symphonies of later centuries, other than being an instrumental

---

52 A six-note scale, here consisting of C–D–E and G–A–B, two intervalically identical groups. Since the B occurs only twice and only in the middle segment, the tune has all of the openness and purity of a pentatonic folk melody. It is in part this quality that brings to mind the African-American spiritual tradition.

53 In 1219 Pope Innocent III and the Fourth Lateran Council made this requirement of Jews and Muslims, saying, "it happens at times that through error Christians have relations with the women of Jews or Saracens, and Jews and Saracens with Christian women. Therefore, that they may not, under pretext of error of this sort, excuse themselves in the future for the excesses of such prohibited intercourse, we decree that such Jews and Saracens of both sexes in every Christian province and at all times shall be marked off in the eyes of the public from other peoples through the character of their dress."

composition. Later in the Baroque, the term often designated a short instrumental piece used as a prelude to or interlude in an opera, ballet, or oratorio (the Pastoral Symphony in Handel's oratorio, *The Messiah*, for example).

This sinfonia, having been written early in the Baroque, still has vestiges of Renaissance era harmony and counterpoint. This is especially apparent in the imitative interplay between the soprano parts at the beginning and in the sudden, unexpected harmonic shifts such as occur in measures 5 and 6 and in measures 12 to 14. As in much contrapuntal music, the biggest challenge is rhythm—staying in the right place when other voices are moving at different times in different directions. Students who try to play be ear or by rote will easily get lost.

154. Heigh Ho Holiday - Anthony Holborne (c. 1545-1602)
(SSATB)

"Heigh Ho Holiday" is a galliard, a dance popular during Holborne's time. (For more detailed information on the galliard, see the notes for #109, "Galliarde," from *Terpsichore*.) This particular galliard is from Holborne's 1599 publication, *Pavans, Galliards, Almains and Other Short Aeirs*. It exhibits many of the characteristics of music from the late English Renaissance, including hemiolas (measures 6–7 in S2); implied metric shifts between 3/4 and 6/8 in the second half; abrupt transitions between major and minor harmonies (F♯ vs F♮ in measures 14 and 15); and picardy thirds at the end of both halves.

Anthony Holborne was an important composer of the Elizabethan era, though little is known about his life. On the title page to *Pavans, Galliards, Almains and Other Short Aeirs* he identifies himself as "Antony Holborne Gentleman and Servant to her most excellent Majestie." One of Holborne's pieces from this book, "The Fairie Round," was included on the Voyager Golden Records, which were sent into space on the Voyager I and Voyager II spacecrafts.

"Heigh Ho Holiday" is both musically and technically challenging. The continuous polyphony, the rhythmic and harmonic twists and turns, and the many running figures all add up to a difficult but rewarding study.

155. Sing You Now After Me - canon in five parts from Pammelia
Thomas Ravenscroft (c. 1582-c. 1635)
(any combination of S, A, T, and B)

The S/T part in this setting moves into the partial-thumb register in the fourth segment, but the transitions are made easier by being at phrase breaks. The F recorder parts are relatively easy.

Sing \ you now after mee, and \ as I sing sing yee, so \ shall we well agree, \ five parts in unity, ding \ dong, ding dong, ding dong, ding dong bell. \ (repeat)

For biographical information about Ravenscroft, see #63, "Miserere Nostri Domine."

156. Cantate Domino Omnis Terra - canon in nine parts
W.A. Mozart (1756-1791)
(any combination of S, A, T, and B)

This canon was written in the summer of 1770. By this time the fourteen-year-old Mozart had already produced 3 masses, 3 operas, 4 piano concertos, 10 string quartets, and a large number of short works for orchestra or vocal ensembles.

The text (*Sing to the Lord, all the earth*) strongly indicates a lively, celebratory tempo. This, together with its busy counterpoint, wide range, and constantly changing rhythmic patterns, not to mention being in nine parts, make it a very challenging work to perform. The canon sounds satisfactory with eight or even seven parts, but with six or fewer the gaps in the counterpoint become increasingly evident. (It actually sounds ok with three voices, though, since the "busy" measures tend to be spaced three bars apart.)

Appendix A - Finger Technique and Fingering Charts

Standard Fingerings for Notes Used in This Volume
Treble Clef Instruments

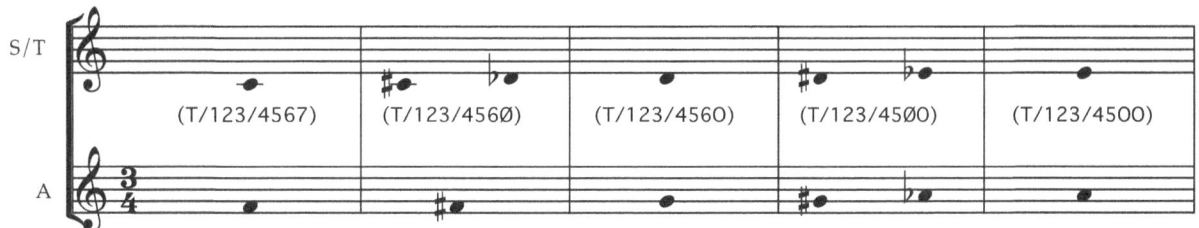

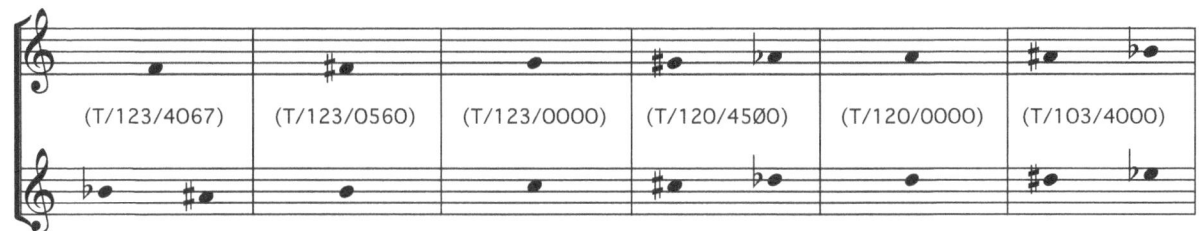

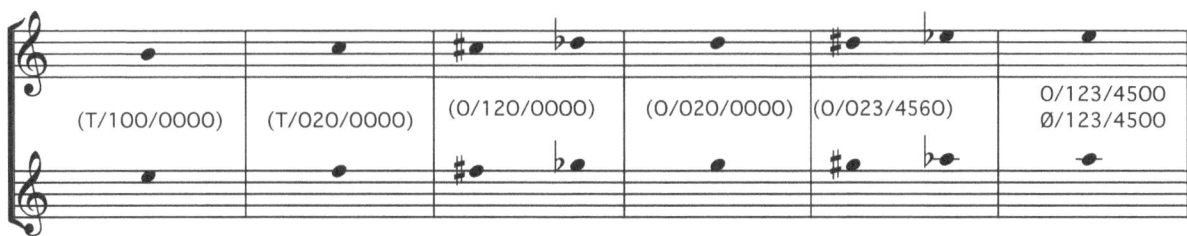

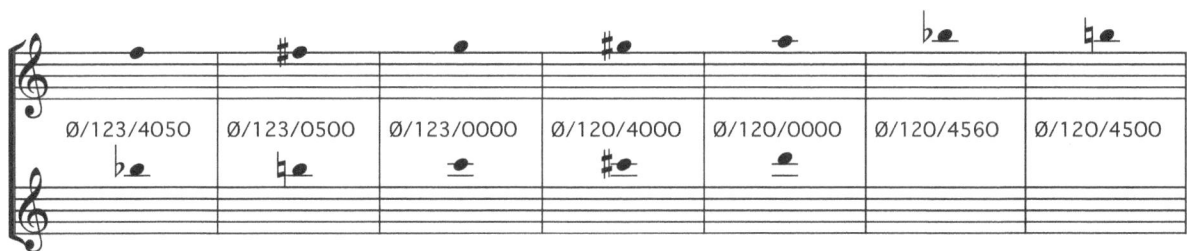

Standard Bass Fingerings for Notes Used in This Volume

There are often significant differences in intonation, especially between brands. Bass recorder players may need to find alternative fingerings or adjust air flow to be in tune with other instruments.

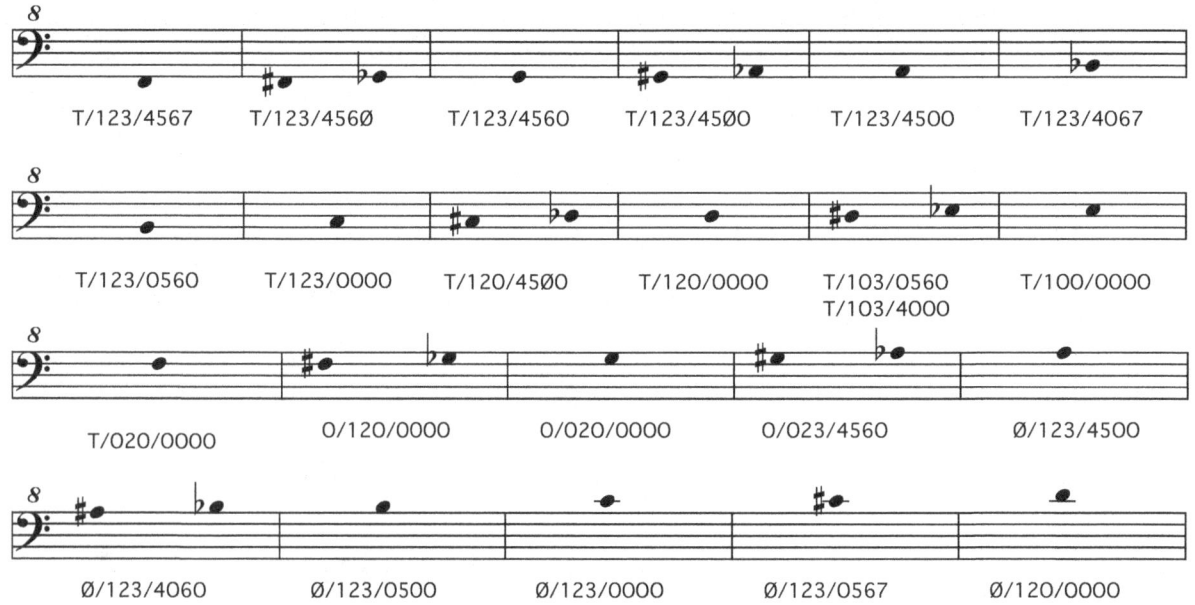

Appendix B - Breathing

In earlier volumes of this series, students were often encouraged to breathe whenever a rest occurred. This was because in most of those pieces, rests tended to occur at the ends of phrases. In some music, rests are used to create short articulation. Examples are the quarter rests in the tenor/bass part of #32, "Roll the Old Chariot Along," the eighth rests in #62, "Bigi Kaiman," and the eighth rests in the tenor and bass parts of #122, "La Raspa." In such situations, it is best to play several notes with a single exhalation, stopping the air flow as needed with the tongue and breathing only as needed.

As students develop physically, they can begin to use diaphragmatic breathing, commonly called "belly breathing." In belly breathing, the abdomen expands as air is drawn deeply into the lungs. Belly breathing can be practiced by breathing with one hand placed on the belly and the other placed on the lower back to feel the expansion. Belly breathing allows one to play long phrases without running out of air.

Another breathing technique is known as "sipping." This involves quickly drawing air into the mouth without inhaling. Often employed during a short rest in a long phrase, it can allow one to reach the end of the phrase without needing to fully inhale.

As noted in earlier volumes, recorder players always breathe through the mouth.

Appendix C - Intonation

While it is possible to tune a recorder by pulling out or pushing in the joints, this practice often results in other notes, particularly those in the high register, going out of tune. Recorder players learn to make slight adjustments in intonation by regulating air flow rather than by changing the bore length: more air raises the pitch, less air lowers it. One must be careful not to exceed the limits, since too much air results in harsh tone, and too little causes weak tone and wavering pitch. In some instances, especially with bass instruments, alternative fingerings may be used. Alternative fingering referred to as "trill fingerings" can be used for fast passages where standard fingerings make for awkward transitions, or also to heighten the harmonic inflection of a note. Several of these are mentioned in the text for pieces in which they might be used.

Bass recorders have notoriously inconsistent intonation, and it can vary from brand to brand. Those playing bass often have to experiment with different fingerings to find one that will harmonize well with the other instruments.

Appendix D - Embouchure and Tonguing

The tip of the mouthpiece rests gently on the lower lip and is not inserted into the mouth. Watch for tell-tale scraping on the top of the mouthpiece that indicates teeth contacting the instrument.

Tonguing is the use of the tongue to articulate notes. The tongue touches the roof of the mouth just behind the front teeth. It never touches the tip of the mouthpiece.

When notes are slurred, the tongue is used only at the beginning and end of the slur. Separate notes are tongued individually. There are two basic methods of tonguing: "hard" tonguing, in which the player articulates as if saying the letter "T" ("tah-tah-taht"); and "soft" tonguing, which uses the letter "D" ("dah-dah-dahd"). Hard tonguing is used when one intends the notes to be clearly articulated, staccato, or accented. Soft tonguing produces a more gentle articulation.

In his *Art of Playing the Flute*, Johann Joachim Quantz (1697–1773) recommended double tonguing with the syllables "did'll" for very fast passages.

Appendix E - The Tenor and Bass Recorders

The point at which a student can begin to play the larger tenor and bass recorders is a matter of hand size and lung capacity. If a student must strain to reach fingers 6 and 7, they should either wait until they have grown more, or they should play these instruments only in pieces with do not require the use of the lowest fingers.

From the standpoint of fingerings, bass recorders with an angled head joint are easier to play than tenors, especially if one uses a neck strap and holds the instrument slightly to the right side of the body (as one would play an alto saxophone). This requires less bending of the right wrist. However, the bass recorder does require a greater lung capacity.

The larger bore of the bass recorder also creates some issues with intonation. Recorder manufacturers typically provide fingering charts showing the bass using the same fingerings as the alto, but in many cases the intonation will not match. A particularly problematic note is E♭. Those playing bass recorder often need to experiment to find fingerings that will be in tune with the smaller instruments.

Another challenge encountered when playing bass recorder is delayed response. It simply takes longer for the larger column of air inside the instrument to vibrate. Bass players need to anticipate the beat slightly, and fast passages are very problematic. Throughout this volume I have adjusted bass parts as needed to facilitate playing.

Appendix F - Indices

Geographical Index

Africa
Botswana: Ha Ba Tshameka (86)
Camaroon: Dance Like a Butterfly (2)
Democratic Republic of the Congo: Ulele (44)
Namibia: Halima Pakasholo (9)
Tanzania: Askari eee (29)
Zimbabwe: Shosholoza (73)

Asia
Russia: Hymn to the Sun (127); Troika (66)

Central America and Caribbean Islands
Costa Rica: Los Esqueletos (124)
Jamaica: Shake the Papaya Down (68); Watah Come a Me Eye (106)
Panama: Julia, Julia, Pela la Yuca (33)
Trinidad and Tobago: Johnny Grotto (5)

Europe
Bohemia: Largo, from Symphony No. 8 (From the New World) (152)
England: Ah Robin, Gentle Robin (56); All Into Service (64); Andalla (118); As I Mee Walked (87); Blow Thy Horne, Hunter (46); British Grenadiers, The (54); Canon 8 Parts: in 4. Retro & Retro (151); Country Gardens (42) Cupid Detected (20); Dry Those Eyes (25); Gathering Peascods (51); Heigh Ho Holiday (154); It Was a Lover and His Lass (130); Jinkin the Jester (148); Joy in the Gates of Jerusalem (144); Jupiter Hymn (125); Laudate Nomen (141); Let's Have a Peale for John Cooke's Soul (140); Levellers and Diggers (101); Love's Content (17); Miserere Nostri Domine (63); Now Is the Month of Maying (149); Now Thanked Be the Great God Pan (146); Pastyme with Good Companye (39); Pinks and Lilies (60); Roll the Old Chariot Along (32); Santiana (13); Sine Nomine (31); Sing We Now Merrily (145); Sing You Now After Me (155); St Agnes Eve (126); Sumer Is Icumin In (143); Up and Down the World Goes Round (70); Viva il Nostra Alcide (95); Wee be Three Poore Mariners (76)
Finland: Finlandia Hymn (92)
France: Alleluia (138); Ballet des Matelotz (113); Chevaliers de la Table Ronde (30); Clair de Lune (120); Galliarde (109); Le Berger Fidèle (26); Leto Leta Concio (115); Marche pour Nérée (75); O Mitissima/Virgo Virginum/Haec Dies (58); Pavane 'Le Bon Vouloir'(150); Vous, Saints Ministres de Seigneur (114); Voyage to the Moon, A (72)
Germany: Ad Cantus Laetitiae (18); Cantata Domino Omnis Terra (156) Da Panem Domine (83); Ein Feste Burg Ist Unser Gott (88); Es Ist Ein' Ros' Entsprungen (96); Feldblumen (77); Freu' Dich des Lebens! (16); Galileo's Epitaph (139); Glaube und Hoffe! (82); Joy and Thanksgiving After the Storm (123); Jubilate Deo (142); Kommt und Laßt Uns Tanzen (81); Lachend Kommt der Sommer (21); Lass Dein' Engel mit Mir Fahren (91); Nun Danket All Gott (97); Schaut Hin! Dort Liegt im Finstern Stall (89); Te Solo Adoro (19); Thebana Bella (147); Wenn Ich Ein Vöglein Wär (59)
Greece: Karaguna (71)
Italy: Alla Matina (Bella Ciao) (36); Ben Venga il Pastor Mio (107); Sinfonia à 5 (153); Sonata Prima (78)
Spain: El Vito (116)
Ukraine: Dalekaya i Blizkaya (117)
Wales: Llywyn Onn (The Ash Grove) (7); Sine Nomine (31)
Unspecified: Estampie (10)

North America

Canada: Au Chant de l'alouette (38); Aylesbury (45); Envoyons de l'avant (24); Nous Étions Trois Soldats (94); Un Canadien Errant (108); We'll Rant and We'll Roar (55)

Mexico: Cielito Lindo (37); El Corrido de Gregario Cortez (90); La Adelita (23); La Jesusita (110); La Raspa (122); Palomita (57)

United States: Ain't Gonna Let Nobody Turn Me Around (131); Amasee (1); Apart (129); Aylesbury (45); By'm Bye (102); Cape Cod Girls (47); Charleston (137); Crazy Blues (128); Daylight, a Musical Expression (119); Dem Bones (99); Down, Down, Down (85); Follow the Drinking Gourd (103); Go Down, Moses (93); Great Big Stars (104); Honor to the Hills (74); Hot Time in the Old Town (100); Jefferson and Liberty (49); Lift Every Voice and Sing (136); Magnetic Rag (134); Mary Had a Baby (14); Michael, Row the Boat Ashore (105); Oh, Watch the Stars (121); Red Iron Ore (35); Shine Like a Morning Star (132); Sing Hallelu! (11); Sit Down, Brother (111); Solace, a Mexican Serenade (135); Star in the East (43); Saint Louis Blues (133); Strike the Bell (112); This Train (98); We Shall Overcome (50); Were You There? (79); Yankee Doodle (53)
Indigenous American: Jump Dance (*Chocktaw*) (4); Sunrise Call (*Zuni*) (6)

Pacific Islands

Australia: Abiyo, Abeyo (3); Click Go the Shears (112)

New Zealand (Aotearoa): Te Aroha (27)

Polynesia: Tongo (8)

South America

Brazil: Boomba (65); Mama Paquita (28); Samba Lele (84)

Suriname: Bigi Kaiman (62)

Unknown

All Joy to Great Caesar (48); At Summer Morn (69); Dayenu (41); Ding dong diggi-diggidong (12); Dundai (22); Echo, The (80); Kum Bachur Atzel (52); Ma Nishtana (40); Ma'oz Tzur (15); Mi Y'malel (61); Round and Round the Earth Is Turning (34); Southerly Wind and Cloudy Sky, A (67)

Thematic Index

Call and Response: Abiyo, Abeyo (3); Amasee (1); Au Chant de l'alouette (38); Dance Like a Butterfly (2); Envoyons de l'avant (24); Ha Ba Tshameka (86); Halima Pakasholo (9); Johnny Grotto (5); Jump Dance (4); Karaguna (71); Santiana (13); Shosholoza (73); Sing Hallelu (11); Sunrise Call (6); Tongo (8)

Canadian History: Au Chant de l'alouette (38); Envoyons de l'avant (24); Nous Étions Trois Soldats (94); Un Canadien Errant (108)

Dance Tunes: Amasee (1); Charleston (137); Country Gardens (42); Dundai (22); Estampie (10); Galliarde (109); Gathering Peascods (51); Jump Dance (4); La Raspa (122); Pavane (150); Pinks and Lilies (60); Troika (66)

Exploration: Au Chant de l'alouette (38); Cape Cod Girls (47); Envoyons de l'avant (24); Nous Étions Trois Soldats (94); Roll the Old Chariot Along (32); Strike the Bell (112); Voyage to the Moon (72)

Festivals: Ad Cantus Laetitiae (*Christmas*) (18); Dayenu (*Passover*) (41); Es Ist Ein' Ros' Entsprungen (*Christmas*) (96); Lass Dein' Engel mit Mir Fahren (*Michaelmas*) (91); Leto Leta Concio (*Christmas*) (115); Mary Had a Baby (*Christmas*) (14); Ma Nishtana (*Passover*) (40); Ma'oz Tzur (*Hanukkah*) (15); Mi Y'malel (*Hanukkah*) (61); Schaut Hin! Dort Liegt im Finstern Stall (*Christmas*) (89); Star in the East (*Christmas*) (43);

Appendices

Indigenous Music:

Africa: Askari eee *(Tanzania)* (29); Halima Pakasholo *(Namibia)* (9); Shosholoza *(Zimbabwe)* (73); Ulele *(Democratic Republic of the Congo)* (44)

Australia: Abiyo, Abeyo (3)

Aotearoa/New Zealand: Te Aroha *(Māori)* (27)

North America: Jump Dance *(Chahta)* (4); Sunrise Call *(Zuni)* (6)

Polynesia: Tongo (8)

Marginalized Composers:

(Traditional music without a composer attribution is not included in this section. See also "Indigenous Music," "Social Justice and Civil Rights," "Festivals," and "Spirituals.")

African-American: Apart (129); Charleston (137); Crazy Blues (128); Daylight: A Musical Expression (119); Dem Bones (99); Lift Every Voice and Sing (136); Magnetic Rag (134); Saint Louis Blues (133); Solace, A Mexican Serenade (135)

Black British: Andalla (118); St Agnes Eve (126)

Jewish: Feldblumen *(19th century Germany)* (77); Sinfonia à 5 *(Renaissance Italy)* (153); Voyage to the Moon (72) *(19th century France)*

Women: Ben Venga il Pastor Mio (107); Feldblumen (77); Le Berger Fidelèle (26); Marche pour Nérée (75); Sonata Prima (78); Wenn Ich Ein Vöglein Wär (59)

Maritime: Cape Cod Girls (47); Roll the Old Chariot Along (32); Santiana (13); Strike the Bell (112); Tongo (8); Wee Be Three Poore Mariners (76)

Medieval Europe: Ad Cantus Laetitiae (18); Estampie (10); Leto Leta Concio (115); O Mitissima/Virgo Virginum/Haec Dies (58); Sumer Is Icumen In (143)

Mexican History: Ceilito Lindo (37) La Adelita (23); La Jesusita (110); Santiana (13)

Myths and Legends: Chevaliers de la Table Ronde (Arthurian legends) (30); Marche pour Nérée (Greek gods) (75)

Nature, Plants, Animals: Bigi Kaiman (62); By'm Bye (102); Country Gardens (42); Feldblumen (77); Gathering Peascods (51); Honor to the Hills (74); Julia, Julia, Pela la Yuca (33); Llywyn Onn (The Ash Grove) (7); Pinks and Lilies (60); Shake the Papaya Down (68)

Renaissance Europe: Ah Robin, Gentle Robin (56); All Into Service (64); As I Mee Walked (87); Ballet des Matelotz (113); Ben Venga il Pastor Mio (107); Blow Thy Horne Hunter (46); Canon 8 Parts (151); Cupid Detected (20); Da Pacem Domine (83); Dry Those Eyes (25); Ein Feste Burg ist Unser Gott (88); El Vito (116) Es Ist Ein' Ros' Entsprungen (96); Galliarde (109); Heigh Ho Holiday (154); It Was a Lover and His Lass (130); Jinkin the Jester (148); Joy in the Gates of Jerusalem (144); Jubilate Deo (142); Lass Dein' Engel mit Mir Fahren (91); Laudate Nomen (141); Let's Have a Peale for John Cooke's Soule (140); Love's Content (17); Miserere Nostri Domine (63); Now Is the Month of Maying (149); Now Thanked Bee the Great God Pan (146); Nun Danket Alle Gott (97); Pastyme with Good Companye (39); Pavane (150); Schaut Hin! Dort Liegt im Finstern Stall (89); Sinfonia à 5 (153); Sing We Now Merrily (145); Sing You Now After Me (155); Up and Down This World Goes Round (70); Vous, Saints Ministres du Seigneur (114); Wee Be Three Poore Mariners (76)

Revolution and Protest Songs: Ain't Gonna Let Nobody Turn Me Around *(civil rights movement)* (131); Alla Matina (Bella Ciao) *(Italian Partisans/WW II)* (36); Finlandia Hymn *(political independence)* (92); La Adelita *(Mexican Revolution)* (23); Levellers and Diggers *(economic inequity in 17th century England)* (101); Mi Y'malel *(Maccabean revolt, 167–160 BCE)* (61); Michael, Row the Boat Ashore *(civil rights movement)* (105); Shosholoza *(anti-Apartheid movement)* (73); Un Canadien Errant *(Lower Canada Rebellion, 1837–1838)* (108); We Shall Overcome *(civil rights movement)* (50)

Reformation: Ein Feste Burg Ist Unser Gott (88); Es Ist Ein' Ros' Entsprungen (96); Lass Dein' Engel mit Mir Fahren (91); Nun Danket Alle Gott (97); Schaut Hin! Dort Liegt im Finstern Stall (89); Vous, Saints Ministres du Seigneur (114)

Rounds and Canons: Ah Robin, Gentle Robin (56); All Into Service (64); Alleluia (138); As I Mee Walked (87); At Summer Morn (69); Canon 8 Parts (151); Cantate Domino Omnis Terra (156); Da Pacem Domine (83); Ding Dong Diggidiggidong (12); Dundai (22); Echo, The (80); Freu' Dich des Lebens! (16); Galileo's Epitaph (139); Jinkin the Jester (148); Joy in the Gates of Jerusalem (144); Jubilate Deo (142); Kommt und Laßt Uns Tanzen (81); Kum Bachur Atzel (52); Lachend Kommt der Sommer (21); Laudate Nomen (141); Let's Have a Peale for John Cooke's Soule (140); Miserere Nostri Domine (63); Now Thanked Bee the Great God Pan (146); Round and Round the Earth Is Turning (34); Shake the Papaya Down (68); Sing We Now Merrily (145); Sing You Now After Me (155); Southerly Wind and Cloudy Sky, A (67); Sumer Is Icumen In (143); Te Solo Adoro (19); Thebana Bella (147); Up and Down This World Goes Round (70); Wee Be Three Poore Mariners (76); Wenn Ich Ein Vöglein Wär (59)

Science:
Acoustics: Echo, The (80)
Astronomy: By'm Bye (102); Clair de Lune (120); Follow the Drinking Gourd (103); Galileo's Epitaph (139); Great Big Stars (104); Hymn to the Sun (127); Jupiter Hymn (125); Oh, Watch the Stars (121); Round and Round the Earth Is Turning (34); Shine Like a Morning Star (132); Up and Down This World Goes Round (70); Voyage to the Moon (72)
Human Physiology: Daylight: A Musical Expression *(eye)* (119); Dem Bones *(skeletal system)* (99); Los Esqueletos *(skeletal system)* (124)
Light: Clair de Lune (120); Daylight: A Musical Expression (119)
Mechanics: Cape Cod Girls (47); Roll the Old Chariot Along (32); Santiana (13); Strike the Bell (112)
Mineralogy: Down, Down, Down (85); Red Iron Ore (35)
Weather: Ceilito Lindo (37); Joy and Thanksgiving After the Storm (123); Southerly Wind and Cloudy Sky, A (67)

Shakespearean: Ah Robin, Gentle Robin (56); Dry Those Eyes (25); It Was a Lover and His Lass (130)

Social Themes: Abiyo, Abeyo *(greeting)* (3); At Summer Morn *(morning song)* (69); Halima Pakasholo *(greeting)* (9); Jefferson and Liberty *(political campaigning)* (49); Kum Bachur Atzel *(morning song)* (52); La Adelita *(gender roles)* (23); Sunrise Call *(morning song)* (6); Te Aroha *(love, hope and peace)* (27)

Social Justice and Civil Rights: Ain't Gonna Let Nobody Turn Me Around *(civil rights movement)* (131); Alla Matina (Bella Ciao) *(Italian rice paddy workers and Partisan movement)* (36); Andalla *(racial discrimination against composer)* (118); Daylight: A Musical Expression *(slavery, disabilities and exploitation)* (119) Down, Down, Down *(workers' rights)* (85); El Corrido de Gregorio Cortez *(ethnic discrimination)* (90); Feldblumen *(gender discrimination against composer)* (77); Hot Time in the Old Town *(Great Chicago Fire, anti-Irish and anti-Catholic discrimination)* (100); Jefferson and Liberty *(slavery, political liberty)* (49); Le Berger Fidelèle *(gender discrimination against composer)* (26); Levellers and Diggers *(economic inequity in 17th century England)* (101); Lift Every Voice and Sing *(civil rights movement)* (136); Marche pour Nérée *(gender discrimination against composer)* (75); Shosholoza *(anti-Apartheid movement)* (73); Un Canadien Errant *(Lower Canada Rebellion, 1837-3188)* (108); We Shall Overcome *(civil rights movement)* (50)

Spirituals: Ain't Gonna Let Nobody Turn Me Around (131); By'm Bye (102); Dem Bones (99); Follow the Drinking Gourd (103); Go Down, Moses (93); Great Big Stars (104); Mary Had a Baby (14); Michael, Row the Boat Ashore (105); Oh, Watch the Stars (121); Sing Hallelu (11); Sit Down, Brother (111); This Train (98) Were You There? (79)

U.S. History: Cape Cod Girls *(whaling)* (47); Daylight: A Musical Expression *(slavery/ post Civil War)* (119); Follow the Drinking Gourd *(slavery)* (103); Go Down, Moses *(underground railroad)* (93); Hot Time in the Old Town *(Great Chicago Fire)* (100); Jefferson and Liberty (49); Lift Every Voice and Sing *(civil rights movement)* (136); Michael, Row the Boat Ashore *(civil rights movement)* (105); Santiana *(Mexican/American War)* (13); Red Iron Ore *(mining, shipping on the Great Lakes)* (35); We Shall Overcome *(civil rights movement)* (50); Yankee Doodle *(Revolutionary War)* (53)

Work Songs: Au Chant de l'alouette (38); Cape Cod Girls (47); Envoyons de l'avant (24); Nous Étions Trois Soldats (94); Red Iron Ore (35); Roll the Old Chariot Along (32); Santiana (13); Shosholoza (73); Strike the Bell (112); Tongo (8)

Acknowledgments

My wife, Susan, who put up with my obsessive arranging and editing at all hours; my daughter, Maret, who reviewed the text for clarity and played the duets along with me; the team at Waldorf Publications, especially Patrice Maynard who pulled all the threads together; Ella LaPointe, whose delightful artwork graces the cover and title pages; Karina Munk Finser, who invited me to be the "traveling minstrel" at Renewal many summers; the colleagues who urged me, some gently, some adamantly, to gather the music I had collected over three decades into a single resource; and, most of all, the children, past, present, and future, for whom the work was done – may music always be part of their lives.